THE SHELLFISH COOK BOOK

THE SHELLFISH COOKBOOK

by MARIAN TRACY

THE BOBBS-MERRILL COMPANY, INC.
A SUBSIDIARY OF HOWARD W. SAMS & CO., INC.
Publishers • INDIANAPOLIS • KANSAS CITY • NEW YORK

PRINTED IN THE UNITED STATES OF AMERICA

DESIGNED BY GERTRUDE AWE/JEAN KRULIS

For
Mary and Kenton Hamaker

Contents

Introduction

I have had a long and joyous love affair with all the beautiful and wonderful shellfish I have encountered in a peripatetic and unmossy life. As in most love affairs, propinquity had much to do with it, that and an unprejudiced palate. I have eaten lobsters in Canada, Maine, and on the Cape; river shrimp in Charleston and at a beautiful mountaintop hotel in Puerto Rico, and all kinds of shrimp in New Orleans; clams up and down the East coast; crabs that were in the Chesapeake *minutes* before; stone crabs in Florida from nearby waters; and oysters native to wherever I have been. All are indeed sublime when eaten at their place of origin, but now they are in markets all over the country, a bounteous plenty arriving by plane, boat and train, fresh, frozen and canned, not only from both our oceans and the Gulf but literally from all the waters of the earth in large and exciting amounts and varieties.

This book is for all who love shellfish and for those, less lucky than I, speaking from a crustacean point of view, eyeing speculatively and adventurously the seafood counters.

All shellfish is a delight to its admirers. It needs only brief cooking and except for such wantonly rich dishes as Lobster Thermidor it is low in calories and cholesterol. In most there is little or no waste and most of it is comparatively inexpensive. The only real drawbacks are in coping with lively, vigorous crabs and lobster (and the lovely ends justify the means) and with the luckily sad few with allergies to some shellfish.

How to eat a lobster is often puzzling at first but simple and fun once you know how. Twist off the claws of the boiled lobster and crack each claw with a lobster cracker, sold as such, or with a sturdy nutcracker, or a wooden mallet, as is used for crabs in Maryland and Virginia. The eager and ingenious have even been known to use a rock or a hammer. Separate the tail from the body by bending it back until it cracks. Break the flippers off the tail and discard. Begin to eat with a fork where the flippers broke off, dipping each piece in melted butter first. Unhinge the back from the body, and discard the back. The tomalley, or liver, found there in the lobster, which turns a lovely yellowish green when cooked, is considered by many to be the best part of the lobster. Open the rest of the lobster by cracking apart sideways with both hands. There is some good meat there. Aficionados put the small wispy claws in their mouth and suck the meat out as daintily as if using a straw. In many American restaurants specializing in seafood, you are given a large and silly bib. This is not necessary. On the other hand, this is not the way it is served at a formal dinner or in a London restaurant. Then it is presented in a more easily eaten fashion and in London, the waiter does all the work very dexterously for you.

When as usual, I started to think about those I should thank who had helped me the most, I got tangled with memories and emotions that include all I have known and loved and meals I have shared. I am thankful that my path crossed that of Bill Finneran again, at a time that made possible this book which has been indeed a labor of love. I have had the help in many ways of these among so many others: Horace Coward, Mary and Kent Hamaker, Cindy and John Watt, Caroline and Herb Ford, Caroline Sauer, Everett Savage, Jean Evans, Jean Lapolla, Arnold Vaught, Clifford Phillips, Laulette Hansen, Bill Moore and Louise Carter.

One · CLAMS

CLAM CURRY CUSTARD

A not-too-stereotyped accompaniment to cocktails.

MENU: *Clam curry custard*
Broiled chicken breasts
Peas
Noodles with butter and poppy seeds
Lemon and angel food cake dessert

CLAM CURRY CUSTARD:

5 eggs
¾ teaspoon salt
1½ teaspoons curry powder
1 tablespoon sherry
¾ cup minced clams
Toast pieces

Put eggs, salt, curry powder, sherry, and 1½ cups water in electric blender. Blend for 15 seconds. Remove, add clams and stir in. Pour into two buttered 9-inch quiche pans or pie tins. Put in larger pans of hot water. Bake in 325° oven for 25 to 30 minutes, or until a knife inserted comes out clean. Cut into diamond, square, or other shapes. Serve warm on pieces of toast cut into the same shapes. Makes 25 to 50 pieces, depending on size.

CLAM PANCAKES

These are fine with cocktails. Make them in a Swedish pancake pan (or in a regular pan, but make them very small). The finished cake should be about 2½ inches in diameter. They are also fine for a late, leisurely breakfast served with bacon curls or Canadian bacon.

MENU: *Clam pancakes, small size*   *Cocktails*
       Shrimp creole (p. 133)
       Bibb lettuce salad
       Charlotte Alice B. Toklas

CLAM PANCAKES:
   1½ cups sifted flour
   2½ teaspoons double-acting baking powder
   ½ teaspoon salt
   Pinch of cayenne
   1 egg, well beaten
   ½ cup milk
   ¾ cup clam juice
   1 can (10½ oz.) minced clams
   2 tablespoons finely chopped chives or parsley
   3 tablespoons melted butter, slightly cooled, or salad
       oil
   More butter or oil

Mix sifted flour, baking powder, salt and cayenne together. Add beaten egg, milk and clam juice. Stir until barely mixed. Add clams, parsley and melted fat. Let stand an hour or two if possible, in order that the batter may "ripen." Grease circles with fat or large pan if used. The batter should be thin. Add more liquid if necessary. Flour varies according to the weather and variety. Heat the pan until water flicked on it dances. Put a spoonful of batter in each depression in the pancake pan so that there is a thin covering. Brown on the first side until the bubbles break, then turn over and brown on the other. Keep warm until needed. These may be made on a regular griddle by using a tablespoon of batter for each cake. Makes about 2½ to 3 dozen small cakes, a dozen regular size.

CLAMS A LA MELANIE

A delicate and delectable beginning to a meal.

MENU: *Clams à la Melanie*
       Steak
       Baked potato with sour cream and chives
       Stewed tomatoes
       Fresh pineapple with Triple Sec

CLAMS A LA MELANIE:
       2 dozen Little Neck clams
       Dash of vinegar
       1 tablespoon parsley, minced
       1 tablespoon chervil, minced
       1 tablespoon onions, minced
       1 teaspoon garlic, minced
       4 tablespoons butter
       Salt, pepper

Rinse clams in cold water. Put into pan with the vinegar and water to cover. Cover and steam just until clams open. Drain clams and remove top half of shell. Blend parsley, chervil, onion and garlic, seasoning and butter. Arrange clams in baking dish. Spread each clam with some of the mixture. Bake for 10 minutes. Serve hot. Serves 4.

STEAMED CLAMS

Besides fresh soft clams, you will need a very large kettle with a cover and at the table extra plates for empty shells.

MENU: *Steamed clams*
Ham
Broccoli with cheese sauce
Sliced tomatoes sprinkled with chives
Pineapple mousse

STEAMED CLAMS:
4 dozen soft clams
1 pound butter, melted
4 tablespoons lemon juice
2 teaspoons Worcestershire sauce

Wash and scrub clams and put in a large kettle with ¾ cup boiling water. Cover and simmer 10 to 12 minutes, or until the shells have opened. Remove clams in clam shells. Put one dozen in a large soup bowl for each person. Serve with a cup of strained clam juice and a dish with a half cup of the melted butter, lemon juice and Worcestershire sauce mixture for each person. A handleless Japanese tea cup is good for this. Serve with oyster forks for dipping into the melted butter mixture. Serves 4.

CHICKEN BROTH WITH MINCED CLAMS

Minced clams add a delicate touch to many dishes, including this broth which is a fine preamble to a meal. It is a good soup to serve on a hot day when the rest of the meal is cold.

MENU: *Chicken broth with minced clams*
Broiled lamb chops
Baked stuffed potatoes
Cold cooked green beans marinated in French dressing
    and sprinkled with chopped black walnuts
Pineapple sherbet

CHICKEN BROTH WITH MINCED CLAMS:
    2 cans (10½ oz.) clear chicken broth
    2 cans (7½ oz.) minced clams and their juice or clam
        juice
    3 tablespoons dry vermouth
    Minced chives or parsley

Heat chicken broth with minced clams and their juice. Add vermouth. Just before serving, sprinkle the top of each bouillon cup or mug with minced chives or parsley. Serves 4. This may also be served cold preceding a hot meal. When serving this broth in a mug, which is a good idea if you wish to serve the first course before coming to the table, be sure to serve a spoon for the minced clams at the bottom or use clam juice without clams.

SPINACH AND CLAM SOUP

Light, delicate and simple to prepare.

MENU: *Spinach and clam soup*
Chicken with tarragon

Broiled tomatoes
New potatoes, boiled in their skins
Chocolate soufflé

SPINACH AND CLAM SOUP:
　　2 packages fresh spinach or 1½ pounds, well washed
　　1 cup heavy cream
　　1 cup light cream
　　2 cups clam juice
　　Dash of grated nutmeg
　　Salt

Cook spinach in one-half cup of boiling water until barely tender. Purée in electric blender or in a food mill. Put the puréed spinach in a pan with light and heavy cream and clam juice. Simmer about 5 to 10 minutes. Add a mere sprinkling of nutmeg and salt to taste. Serve hot or cold. Serves 4.

NEW ENGLAND CLAM CHOWDER

New England clam chowder, which is the one I like, is very different from the Manhattan variety. That one has tomatoes and other vegetables in it instead of milk.

MENU: *New England clam chowder*
　　　Asparagus salad
　　　Fresh pineapple chunks with banana liqueur

NEW ENGLAND CLAM CHOWDER:
　　¼ pound diced salt pork
　　1 onion, sliced
　　4 medium-sized raw potatoes, diced
　　1 quart milk
　　Salt, pepper

2 dozen raw clams, drained and chopped fine, or 2 cans
(7½ oz.) minced clams

Sauté salt pork in a deep saucepan, and cook onion in the fat
until it turns golden brown. Add potatoes, milk, salt and pepper. Cook until potatoes are tender. Add the clams and juice.
If fresh clams are used, they should be steamed open, chopped,
and the liquid strained through cheesecloth into the soup.
Many think this is better if refrigerated for a day before serving, but it may be served immediately. Serve pilot crackers
with the chowder. Serves 4.

MANHATTAN CLAM CHOWDER

This chowder has as many adherents as the New England kind,
perhaps, but I am not one of them. However, this is a democ-
racy, and you may choose your own.

MENU: *Manhattan clam chowder*
Broiled hamburgers
Broiled stuffed mushrooms
Risi pisi
Apple pie

MANHATTAN CLAM CHOWDER:
¼ cup bacon drippings or other fat
1 medium-sized onion, chopped
1 large carrot, peeled and chopped
3 medium-sized raw potatoes, diced
1 pint chopped clams and juice
1 large can, 1 lb., 12 oz., can tomatoes
Salt, pepper
½ teaspoon celery seed

Sauté onions and carrots in the fat in a soup pan over low heat. Add the potatoes and boiling water to cover. Cover and cook until potatoes are tender, about 10 minutes. Add tomatoes and clams, clam juice and seasonings. Bring to a boil, turn heat down immediately. Simmer for 10 to 15 minutes. Add more seasoning if desired. Serve in heated soup plates with toasted pilot crackers. Serves 4.

FRIED LITTLE NECK CLAMS OR MANINOSE

Clam fritters may be made with canned whole clams or from fresh Little Neck or maninose. If fresh clams are used, many people put them in a bucket of water for half a day until they have worked out all the sand, which they do by opening and closing in the water. Others prefer to open them and slit the necks or snouts and wash the sand out.

MENU: *Fried Little Neck clams or maninose*
Green beans
French fried onions
Field salad (lamb's lettuce)
Danish red pudding

FRIED LITTLE NECK CLAMS OR MANINOSE:
2 dozen clams, drained thoroughly (see above)
3 eggs, beaten
6 to 8 tablespoons flour
Salt, pepper
Fat for frying

Mix eggs, flour, salt and pepper into a batter. The amount of flour will depend upon the size of the eggs. The batter should not be too thick. Dip clams in this, a few at a time. Fry in deep fat heated to 375°, until golden brown. Drain on paper towels and serve. Serves 3 or 4, depending on appetites.

CLAMS CASINO

Clams or oysters may be used interchangeably in this recipe and, less traditionally, so can mussels.

MENU: *Clams casino*
Potato soufflé with chives
Celery Victor (celery hearts cooked in chicken broth, drained, marinated and chilled)
Gingerbread with lemon sherbet

CLAMS CASINO:
2 dozen medium-size cherrystone clams on the half shell
½ cup (1 stick) butter, softened
⅓ cup finely chopped green onions
1 pimiento, finely chopped
3 tablespoons finely chopped parsley
Juice of 1 lemon
Salt, pepper, dash of cayenne
6 slices of bacon, each cut in fours
4 pie tins, each half filled with rock salt

Preheat the oven to 450°. Arrange 6 clams in their shells on each pan of rock salt. Mix butter, onions, pimiento, parsley, lemon juice, salt, pepper, cayenne. Put a spoonful of this mixture on each clam and top with a piece of bacon. Bake until bacon is brown, 5 to 8 minutes. Serve 6 to a person. Garnish with lemon wedges. Serves 4.

CLAM FRITTERS

These may be made with fresh or canned clams. Little Neck clams, which are most often used in this dish, nowadays mostly come from around Chesapeake Bay, where they are called maninose. The New England beds have been overworked, and in those cold waters it takes five years for clams to grow two inches, which is the legal size. In the Chesapeake, with year-round feeding a clam attains the same size in a year and a half.

MENU: *Clam fritters*
Broccoli soufflé
Tomato aspic
Frozen orange sherbet pie

CLAM FRITTERS:
2 cups ground or minced clams, fresh or canned, drained
4 tablespoons cracker crumbs
2 eggs
Salt, pepper
¾ cup bacon drippings

Mix clams and cracker crumbs. Add eggs and mix thoroughly. Season with salt and pepper. Pat into thin cakes, 3 to 4 inches in diameter. Heat bacon fat in skillet and sauté fritters on each side until a light golden brown. Serve immediately with dill pickles on the side. Serves 4.

DEVILED CLAMS

Clams take to many stuffings and many seasonings, usually those on the lusty side.

MENU: *Deviled clams*
Corn on the cob
Baked potatoes
Escarole salad
Wine sherbet

DEVILED CLAMS:

2 dozen clams or quahogs, opened on the half shell
(save 2 tablespoons juice)
1 cup herb-seasoned stuffing, or ½ cup Colonna seasoned bread crumbs
⅓ cup chopped parsley
2 tablespoons finely chopped green pepper
2 teaspoons Worcestershire sauce
2 tablespoons lemon juice
Salt
Dash of cayenne
2 tablespoons melted butter

Mix the crumbs or stuffing with parsley, green pepper, Worcestershire sauce, lemon juice, salt, cayenne, melted butter,
and clam juice. Divide among the two dozen clams. Put a
spoonful on each and smooth it out. Bake at 350° for 20 minutes or until lightly browned. Serve a half dozen each to 4
people.

CLAM PIE

Some make a sturdy version with potatoes; others prefer to
have the clams in a cream sauce, and so do I.

MENU: *Clam pie*
Corn on the cob

Asparagus salad
Peach ice cream

CLAM PIE:

Unbaked pastry for two-crust pie
4 tablespoons butter
1 medium onion, finely chopped
½ medium green pepper, chopped
3 tablespoons flour
2 dozen fresh clams and their juice, or 2 cans minced
   clams and juice, or 2 cans whole clams and juice
1 cup light cream
Pepper, if necessary

Melt butter and sauté onion and pepper until limp. Sprinkle with flour and stir until it is absorbed. Add clams and their juice a little at a time, stirring until smooth and thickened. Add cream and cook until that, too, is smooth and thickened. Pour the mixture in uncooked pie shell. Cover with top crust and prick the pie dough. Bake in a 425° oven about 20 minutes or until nicely brown. Serves 4.

PASTA WITH WHITE CLAM SAUCE

The Italians, who dress all shapes of pasta with all kinds of sauces, include this in their list of basic sauces. It may be made with canned whole or chopped clams. It is, of course, better when made with freshly shucked clams. I prefer to have my fishman shuck them.

MENU: *Pasta with white clam sauce*
Garden lettuce, tomato and hard-cooked egg salad
Italian bread
Apple charlotte

PASTA WITH WHITE CLAM SAUCE:

    1 clove garlic, minced

    3 tablespoons olive oil

    1 tablespoon finely chopped parsley

    3 whole anchovies or 2 teaspoons anchovy paste

    3 dozen shucked Little Neck clams and juice, or 3 cans
       whole clams

    1 hot red pepper pod, crushed

    1 pound pasta, preferably one of the fine ones.

Cook garlic in oil with parsley, slowly, being careful not to let it get black and bitter. (If it does, throw it out and start all over.) Add clam juice, anchovies and pepper pod. Simmer for 5 minutes. Add whole clams and simmer for one-half minute only. Pour over cooked and drained pasta and serve. Serves 4–6.

PASTA WITH RED CLAM SAUCE

Both white and red clam sauces belong to a classic group of Italian sauces that are made with any kind of shellfish. Red clam sauce is used mostly on pasta, but sometimes on polenta, sometimes on rice.

MENU: *Pasta with red clam sauce*
       Cold marinated green beans with black walnuts
       Italian bread
       Caramel custard

PASTA WITH RED CLAM SAUCE:

    3 tablespoons olive oil

    1 small onion, chopped

    1 clove garlic, chopped fine

    1 large can, 1 lb. 12 oz., tomatoes, preferably Italian

plum tomatoes, which are sweeter. Strain to remove
the seeds before adding to the pan
1 can Italian tomato paste
⅓ cup finely chopped parsley
1 teaspoon oregano
1 teaspoon salt
2 cups chopped clams, fresh or canned, or 6 hard-
shelled crabs and ½ pound crab meat or 1 2-pound
lobster, cut up
1 pound pasta, any shape

Sauté onion and garlic in oil and transfer to a large pot. (Aluminum or iron turns tomatoes dark.) Add tomatoes, tomato
paste, and four paste cans of water, then the parsley and seasonings. Cook over low heat 2 to 3½ hours. Stir slowly from
time to time with a wooden spoon, adding more water as
needed. At the end of the time, the sauce should be rich and
voluptuously smooth and thick, but not too thick to pour on
the pasta. Add shellfish and cook briefly. Have a large kettle
of water boiling, and just before serving add the pasta and
cook until tender but not mushy. There should be some re-
sistance to the teeth. Drain. Serves 6 generously.

CLAM MOUSSE

For a sultry, summer day. Check the seasoning carefully. A
mousse blots it up in a surprising way.

MENU: *Clam mousse*
       Zucchini and tomato casserole
       Baked apples filled with ginger marmalade

CLAM MOUSSE:
       2 envelopes unflavored gelatin

1 cup boiling chicken broth
4 teaspoons lemon juice
1 tablespoon parsley clusters
1 cup diced cucumbers
1 teaspoon dry tarragon
2 cans, 7½ oz., minced clams and their juice
1 cup sour cream
Salt, pepper

Put gelatin in the container of an electric blender with boiling chicken broth, lemon juice, parsley clusters, cucumber and tarragon. Cover and blend about 1 minute. Remove from container and add clams, their juice and the sour cream. Season to taste. Turn into a 5-cup mold and chill until firm. Serves 4.

A CLAMBAKE IN A KETTLE

At one time a clambake was a seaside picnic much like an oyster roast except that clams and lobsters were steamed instead of oysters. This kind is still being held. They have the same long pits, seaweed, etc., but now the inlanders can have them, too, with live clams and live lobsters sent by fast freight or air express. One misplaced Easterner, yearning for shellfish, had one for his inland neighbors and the party began as adventure and ended with much gastronomic bliss. Corn is bought locally.

MENU: *Steamed clams*
Steamed lobsters
Steamed green corn
Melted butter
Watermelon

Put a layer of seaweed in the bottom of a large kettle or use the container in which clams and lobsters are shipped. One firm, I think, sends seaweed; if not, use dampened cornhusks. On seaweed or cornhusks, place the live lobsters, grasping from behind. (Some have their claws wedged.) Cover with another layer of seaweed, place corn in husks and top with more seaweed, then a layer of clams and another layer of seaweed. Steam over an outdoor fireplace over hot coals. The time will vary. It may be about ½ hour. When the clams open, start with them. Melted butter is served with the clams and they are dipped by oyster forks in butter and then eaten dripping. By the time the clams have been eaten, the lobsters will be done and be ready for more melted butter as will the corn, and the corn will need salt, too. It is a good way of cutting down on our surpluses but not, of course, the night you go on a diet. With the lobsters, serve crackers to break the claws and more oyster forks to get the meat out. Lobsters can be bought in varying numbers, depending upon how lavish and hospitable you feel. Eight lobsters will serve eight and the clams are in proportion, more or less.

GEODUCK WITH SPINACH IN TOMATOES

Geoduck pronounced gooey duck, is an enormous clam found on the Pacific Coast. They sometimes weigh as much as 6 pounds each. They are submerged most of the time except for an hour or so at low tide. It is rather sporting to dig them because the clams are very smart and can get out of the way fast. They are spotted by their snouts which flop around the sand. The digger must sneak up and dig fast. The snout is skinned and chopped and used in chowder or such dishes as this. Many Pacific Coast dwellers think the body, which is sometimes sliced, breaded and fried, should be chopped, too. They can be tough. If the sport does not appeal, use canned minced clams. Pour boiling water over the scrubbed geoduck, pull the shell off and the skin from the neck and the body. Grind neck and slice the body and fry (see above) or chop this, too.

MENU: *Geoducks with spinach in tomatoes*
Hominy soufflé
Tossed greens with Roquefort dressing
Baked lemon turnovers (bought)

GEODUCKS WITH SPINACH IN TOMATOES:
4 large tomatoes
1 cup or more chopped spinach, fresh or frozen
1 cup chopped geoduck or 1 can, 7½ oz., minced clams, drained
1 teaspoon grated lemon peel
Salt, pepper
Pinch of nutmeg
½ cup sour cream

Cut tops off tomatoes, rinse under cold water to get the seeds out. Drain upside down. Mix spinach, clams, seasonings and sour cream. Fill tomatoes, being careful not to pack too tightly. Bake in a 350° oven until the skins wrinkle. Serve warm. On a hot day, they may be chilled. Serves 4.

Two · CRABS AND CRAB MEAT

MARYLAND CRAB SOUP

In Maryland, the soup that precedes an orgy of steamed hard-shell crabs (p. 39) is somewhat of an orgy itself, not a dainty prelude to a meal. In the soup there are crabs, of course. If you are near to the source, the whole crab is put into the soup which has a base of chicken or beef (beef is the favorite) and bacon and some of all the fresh vegetables you can find at crab time around the Chesapeake. If making this where there is no supply of fresh crab, canned or frozen may be used, with frozen cracked Dungeness crab claws put in to add an authentic clutter. This is not the kind of dish that you whip up for a few. It is made when there are going to be 10 to 12. A streamlined version may be made by starting with a large bag of frozen mixed vegetables, plus some canned tomatoes, potatoes, onions, and cabbage, a few bouillon cubes or beef stew meat and, naturally, crabs.

> 1 pound shin beef, in one piece
> ¼ pound bacon, unsliced

6 steamed crabs
3 tomatoes, quartered
3 potatoes, peeled and diced
1 onion, chopped
1 cup whole-kernel corn, cut from the cob or frozen or
    canned
1 cup lima beans
1 cup string beans, cut in pieces
2 stalks celery, diced
2 carrots, diced
1 cup finely shredded cabbage
¼ cup chopped parsley
4 quarts water
¾ cup beer
1 teaspoon mustard
4 tablespoons butter or margarine, melted
2 teaspoons seafood seasoning or Worcestershire sauce

Break off claws from bodies of crabs, discard small ones and crack large ones. Pull off back shell, remove gills or devil and face of crab (eyes and sandbag should come off with shell). Break crab in half and cut across each half, parallel to shells, but do not remove meat. Combine these body pieces, large claws, bacon, beef, vegetables, beer, water and seasoning. Simmer 1 to 2 hours. French bread and beer accompany it. Serves 10–12.

SHE-CRAB SOUP

In Charleston, South Carolina, men still go through the streets calling "she-crab, she-crab." These crabs are bought for soup. It's the eggs in she-crab that give the soup that special touch. It is not realistic to give a recipe calling for "she-crabs" anywhere except in Charleston, but this is an acceptable approximation. Even Charlestonians have been known to use this one.

MENU: *She-crab soup*
Roast leg of lamb with anchovies
Fried rice
Tomato aspic with cottage cheese layer
Pistachio ice cream

SHE-CRAB SOUP:
1 quart half cream and half milk
1 teaspoon grated lemon peel
⅛ teaspoon mace
1 pound white crab meat (and crab eggs)
½ stick butter
¼ cup cracker crumbs
4 tablespoons dry sherry
Salt, pepper to taste
3 hard-cooked egg yolks (if she-crab is not available)

Heat half-and-half in the top of a double broiler with mace and lemon peel. Allow to simmer for a few minutes. Add crab meat and butter and cook for 15 minutes. Add cracker crumbs to thicken, salt, pepper and sherry. Allow to stand for a few minutes to ripen. When serving, put crab eggs in each bowl. Or, if you have not been able to get she-crabs, crumble a little egg yolk in the bottom of each warm soup bowl. Serves 4-6.

CRAB CAKES

All crab cakes around the Chesapeake Bay area, in fancy places and in plain, are good. It's just that some are better than others. The ingredients vary slightly. Some use backfin crab meat, some use regular, and some use the dark meat from claws. Each kind of crab meat has its adherents. Most agree that like pie dough, the less the crab meat is handled, the tenderer the cake. I prefer lump crab meat barely mixed, and no bread crumbs added.

MENU: *Crab cakes*
Corn pudding
Cole slaw
French bread
Watermelon

CRAB CAKES:
1 pound crab meat
2 tablespoons mayonnaise
1 tablespoon prepared mustard
1 teaspoon Worcestershire sauce
1 tablespoon finely chopped parsley
1/4 teaspoon salt
1 large egg
Butter
Oil

Pick over crab meat, removing the membranes, but handling it as little as possible. Mix all other ingredients except the fat together in a small bowl. Add to the crab meat, and barely mix, using a spoon and not your hands. Make into cakes about 2 1/2 inches in diameter, again handling as little as possible. The cakes should be rather flat. Sauté in a mixture of butter and oil about a half inch deep. Makes 8 to 9 crab cakes.

DEVILED CRAB

Crab cakes and deviled crab and crab imperial are variants of the same recipe, with deviled crab being the most robust.

It used to be served in the original shell until the health department started tut-tutting around. Now restaurants are supposed to put deviled crab in an edible shell or a plastic one, but here and there, there is a rather carefree approach to the law, and you will still find deviled crab being put in crabshells. Of course, in your own home, you are privileged to have all the bacteria you want.

MENU: *Deviled crabs*
French fried eggplant
Red cabbage slaw with Roquefort dressing
Pineapple sherbet with fresh strawberries

DEVILED CRAB:
1 pound crab meat
2 tablespoons minced onion
3 tablespoons butter
3 tablespoons mayonnaise
Salt and pepper
1 teaspoon dry mustard
Dash of cayenne
1 tablespoon lemon juice
1 egg
1 tablespoon minced parsley
Bread crumbs (not obligatory)
More butter (not obligatory)

Pick over crab meat, removing membranes. Cook the onion in butter. Remove from fire, add salt, pepper, mustard, cayenne, lemon juice, egg, parsley, and crab meat. Toss lightly together. Pile loosely in crabshells or ramekins. If a crisp crust is desired, sprinkle the tops with bread crumbs and dot with butter. Bake in a 350° oven about 15 minutes or until browned. Serves 4 to 6.

CRAB IMPERIAL

This is a delicate and elegant version of deviled crab which is served for festive occasions. It is baked and served in baking shells available in most places that handle good cooking equipment. Some versions are made with a cream sauce base, others with mayonnaise.

MENU: *Crab imperial*
Broccoli soufflé
Drop biscuits
Hearts of lettuce with Russian dressing
Brandied peaches

CRAB IMPERIAL:
½ cup mayonnaise
1 tablespoon Worcestershire sauce
2 tablespoons finely chopped green pepper
1 whole pimiento, chopped
½ teaspoon dry mustard
½ teaspoon salt
1 egg
1 pound lump or backfin crabmeat
Butter
Bread crumbs

Mix mayonnaise, Worcestershire sauce, pimiento, green pepper, mustard and salt. Stir in the egg. Add lump crab meat which has been picked over for pieces of membrane, but not pulled into shreds. The lumps should remain lumps. Heap into four baking shells and round, patting lightly. Sprinkle tops stingily with bread crumbs and dot with butter. Bake in a 350° oven about 20 minutes, or until lightly browned on top. Serves 4.

CRAB NORFOLK

This is fresh lump crab meat at its most blissful best and I'm afraid it would not taste at all the same made from frozen or canned crab. It is filling in a sneaky way. It is served sizzling hot, and few but the most rugged and stalwart eaters can eat much else. Usually sliced tomatoes are served in individual salad bowls with crab Norfolk. I like to sprinkle them with finely chopped basil.

MENU: *Crab Norfolk*
Sliced fresh tomatoes, sprinkled with finely chopped fresh basil
Salt sticks
Tangerine sherbet

CRAB NORFOLK:
1 pound lump or backfin crab meat
½ cup (1 stick) butter
1 tablespoon vinegar or lemon juice
Salt, a shake of cayenne pepper, a speck of red

Pick over crab meat and remove any membranes, but do not pull it to pieces. Divide into four shallow individual casseroles, preferably metal. Melt butter, mix with vinegar or lemon juice and seasonings. Pour over crab meat and heat briefly in the oven or under a broiler until sizzling. Rush to the table. This is much more filling that it looks, so just a salad, rolls, and a dessert make a meal for almost anyone. Serves 4.

CRAB IN SCALLOP SHELLS

Besides liking variety in my food, I like variety in its presentation, not a plate with meat, potatoes and green vegetable appearing in the same guise night after night. Some nights I like my meat skewered, some nights baked in individual dishes, and sometimes cooked with vegetables in a casserole. I even like to vary the dishes for individual servings. Scallop shells may be used for other foods.

MENU: *Crab in scallop shells*
Noodles with butter and poppy seeds
Romaine with sliced raw mushrooms and French dressing
Canned green gage and purple plums

CRAB IN SCALLOP SHELLS:
1 pound crab meat
½ cup stale white bread soaked in
½ cup heavy cream
2 small white onions, minced
2 tablespoons butter
2 tablespoons flour
1 cup white wine
1 tablespoon parsley, finely chopped
½ cup Gruyère cheese
Pinch of cayenne pepper
Salt
Bread crumbs
Clam broth or juice

Pick over the crab meat, removing any bits of membrane. Blend into soaked bread crumbs. Set aside. Sauté onions until pale yellow and sprinkle on flour. Moisten with 1 cup clam broth, stirring constantly until thickened. Add white wine, parsley, salt, cayenne pepper, stirring over heat for 5 minutes. Remove from heat. Fold in crab meat and fill 6 shells, cover with grated cheese, then with bread crumbs. Bake in 350° oven until golden brown. Serves 4.

CRAB RISOTTO

At one time, here in the United States not so long ago, rice was mostly cooked and served as a natural way of life only by Southerners and recent arrivals from around the Mediterranean. Others served it as a dull and sticky substitute for potatoes, which were much preferred. Now almost everyone is learning that it is a starting point for many, fascinating dishes of different ethnic groups.

MENU: *Crab risotto*
Hearts of lettuce with Russian dressing
Raspberry pie

CRAB RISOTTO:
1 cup uncooked rice
2 medium-sized onions, chopped
3 tablespoons olive oil
2 8-ounce cans tomato sauce
⅓ cup chopped parsley
1 clove garlic
1 pound fresh crab meat, or 2 7½-ounce cans crab meat
picked over and membranes removed
Grated Parmesan cheese

Cook the rice with onions in olive oil until rice is translucent and onion pale yellow. Add tomato sauce, cover and steam until done. Add parsley, garlic, crab meat and grated Parmesan cheese. Cook over a very low flame until all the ingredients are hot and the cheese has melted into them. Serves 4.

CRAB FLAKES WITH BROCCOLI

Somewhat like Chicken Divan.

MENU: *Crab flakes with broccoli*
Garden lettuce with French dressing
Orange ice with Danish butter cookies

CRAB FLAKES WITH BROCCOLI:

2 packages frozen broccoli, cooked according to package directions, or 1 bunch fresh broccoli, trimmed and cooked until tender
1 pound fresh crab meat or 2 cans 7½ oz. or 2 packages frozen crab meat
1 can condensed cream of mushroom soup, undiluted
2 tablespoons sherry
¾ cup freshly grated yellow cheese

Arrange cooked broccoli in a shallow casserole. Remove membranes from crab meat; strew meat on top of the broccoli. Mix mushroom soup with sherry and cheese and pour on top. Allow some broccoli to show around the edges. Bake in an oven preheated to 350° until well heated and slightly brown on top, about 15 to 20 minutes. Serves 4.

CRAB MEAT AND EGGPLANT CASSEROLE

Eggplant serves as a splendid foil for rich, lusty sauces. It is also a delicate complement to such shellfish as crab, shrimp, or clams. Each flavor is enhanced and set off by the other.

MENU: *Crab meat and eggplant casserole*
Bibb lettuce and herb dressing
Hot rolls
Slices of orange cake topped with scoops of orange sherbet

CRAB MEAT AND EGGPLANT CASSEROLE:
>   1 large eggplant, peeled and diced
>   Juice of 1 lemon
>   6 medium-sized ripe tomatoes, diced, seeded and
>   drained, or 2 cans tomato sauce
>   3 eggs, beaten
>   1 pound crab meat, flaked and membranes removed
>   Salt, pepper
>   ½ cup bread crumbs
>   3 tablespoons butter

Sprinkle eggplant with lemon juice, cover with water and cook over medium heat until barely tender, about 10 minutes. Drain and put into a baking dish, put a layer of crab meat on it, and pour over it the tomatoes, or tomato sauce, and eggs. Sprinkle the top with bread crumbs and dot with butter. Bake in a 350° oven 20 to 25 minutes. Serves 4.

BAKED POTATOES WITH CRAB MEAT SAUCE

Robust and filling, yet delicate in flavor.

MENU: *Baked potatoes with crab meat sauce*
>   *Spinach*
>   *Mimosa salad*
>   *Corn toast*
>   *Orange fritters*

BAKED POTATOES WITH CRAB MEAT SAUCE:
>   4 large Idaho potatoes of even size, scrubbed and
>   greased
>   3 tablespoons butter
>   3 tablespoons flour
>   1½ cups milk

1 tablespoon capers
1 tablespoon finely chopped parsley
½ pound fresh or canned crab meat, picked over
Salt, pepper

Bake potatoes at least an hour or more in a moderate oven until they feel soft when punched. Melt the butter and add flour. Stir until smooth and slightly dry. Add milk gradually, stirring constantly until mixture is smooth and has thickened. Then add capers, parsley, crab meat, salt and pepper. Break the potatoes open and pour one quarter of the sauce on each. Serve immediately. Serves 4.

CRAB CASSEROLE

This is superb when made with fresh lump crab meat, but good with frozen or canned.

MENU: *Crab casserole*
Fresh asparagus with butter and lemon
Rice fritters
Tomato salad
Fresh figs and cream

CRAB CASSEROLE:
1 small onion, chopped fine
2 tablespoons butter
¼ teaspoon sugar
2 cups light cream or half-and-half
1 tablespoon Worcestershire sauce
1 tablespoon cornstarch diluted with a little milk
1 pound lump crab meat or 2 6½-ounce cans
1 tablespoon capers, drained
1 tablespoon finely chopped parsley
2 tablespoons finely grated Parmesan cheese

Brown the onion in butter. Add sugar, cream, Worcestershire sauce, cornstarch and milk. Simmer and stir until thickened. Add crab meat and capers and barely mix with a wide-pronged fork until heated through. Turn into a shallow buttered baking dish. Sprinkle with parsley and cheese. Put into a 350° oven and brown for 15 to 20 minutes. Serves 4.

CRAB MEAT SOUFFLE

In a crab meat soufflé, canned crab tastes very good. It makes an elegant and impromptu dish right from the kitchen shelves.

MENU: *Crab soufflé*
Broccoli with lemon juice
Bacon biscuits
Pineapple upside-down cake

CRAB MEAT SOUFFLÉ:

½ pound fresh crab meat or 1 can 6½ oz., flaked
3 tablespoons butter
3 tablespoons flour
1 cup chicken broth
3 eggs, separated
1 tablespoon sherry
Salt, pepper

Melt butter and stir in flour, salt and pepper. Add broth slowly and cook until thick. Remove from stove, add egg yolks, sherry and crab meat. Whip whites until stiff. Fold into crabmeat mixture gently. Pile into four individual greased casseroles or a 2-quart one. Bake in medium oven, 325°, until brown and springy to the touch. Serves 4.

SIZZLING DUNGENESS CRAB LEGS

This is a voluptuous dish, popular on the West Coast and not unlike East Coast Crab Norfolk.

MENU: *Sizzling Dungeness crab legs*
French fried potatoes
French bread
White wine
Pear and ginger sherbet

SIZZLING DUNGENESS CRAB LEGS:
1½ pounds crab legs, bought shelled
⅓ cup melted, unsalted butter
⅓ cup lemon juice
Paprika

Marinate the crab legs for two hours in butter and lemon juice. Broil until slightly charred. Dust with paprika and serve with the heated marinade. Serves 4.

FRIED SOFT-SHELL CRABS

Soft-shell crabs are hard-shell crabs which have sloughed off their tight old shell and have not yet had time to grow a new one in a larger size. It takes about 48 hours, which is what makes this delicacy rare and expensive most places.

MENU: *Fried soft-shell crabs with tartar sauce*
Green beans amandine
Potato pancakes with sour cream
Hot popovers
Broiled grapefruit halves with honey

FRIED SOFT-SHELL CRABS:
> 12 to 16 soft-shell crabs, depending on size
> Salt, pepper
> Flour
> Butter

Clean crabs by removing spongy substance under the pointed flap and the feathery gills on either side. Then cut across the front to remove eyes and sandbag. Sprinkle lightly with salt, pepper. Dip in flour and either fry in butter ½ inch deep or deep fry, according to taste. Serves 4.

BROILED SOFT-SHELL CRABS AMANDINE

Soft-shell crabs, which have such a brief interval in which to be caught, marketed and eaten, are one of the best of our native delicacies. Crabs are usually bought alive, but in such a weakened condition that they hardly seem so. They appear almost to be ghost crabs. Even one as timid as I am does not mind handling them. They are incapable of fighting back.

MENU: *Broiled soft-shell crabs amandine*
> *Sliced yellow squash, baked with butter and finely chopped onions*
> *Romaine lettuce with Roquefort dressing*
> *Fresh pineapple halves with sherbet*

BROILED SOFT-SHELL CRABS AMANDINE:
> ½ cup butter
> 2 tablespoons lemon juice
> Salt, pepper, cayenne
> 8 soft-shell crabs
> Flour
> 2 tablespoons butter

⅓ cup slivered blanched almonds
Lemon quarters

Clean crabs and remove spongy material under the pointed flaps at each side. (See recipe for Fried Soft-Shell Crabs, p. 31.) Melt butter. Add lemon juice and cayenne pepper. Sprinkle crabs with salt and pepper and roll in butter sauce. Dust with flour and place on a broiler rack. Place under a broiler flame and broil until browned on both sides. Meanwhile, sauté almonds in the rest of the butter till lightly brown. Pour over broiled crabs on the serving dish or platter. Garnish with lemon quarters. Serves 4. When crabs are on home ground, reasonably plentiful and not too expensive, more are eaten.

BOILED FLORIDA STONE CRABS WITH MELTED BUTTER

These are the most ambrosial, perhaps, of all shellfish. I do, indeed, love fresh Maine or Canadian lobsters and I would not be faithless to the blue crabs of the Chesapeake. But these are almost out of this world. Only the claws are used, which are a brilliant lobster color with a bold, splashing dash of bright black on the tip. Once you have cracked them, you will understand how they got their name. They are scarce and costly, and the conservation laws cruel-sounding. When the crabs are caught, you are permitted to remove one claw, then you must toss the crab and its remaining claw back in the water to grow another one.

MENU: *Boiled stone crabs with melted butter*
Watercress and endive salad
French bread
Strawberry meringues

BOILED STONE CRABS WITH MELTED BUTTER:
        16 stone crab claws
        1 cup melted butter

Boil the claws about 20 minutes. Take a cloth folded in several thicknesses. Lay a hot claw on this cloth and crack each of the three sections with a wooden mallet or other strong instrument. Give it a good crack. The shell is sometimes more than ⅛ inch thick, and it takes a real blow to penetrate. Arrange cracked claws on a plate, four for each serving. Serve with plenty of melted butter. Serves 4.

COLD FLORIDA STONE CRABS WITH MUSTARD SAUCE

One might murmur, reverently, "All *this*, and heaven too!" when eating Florida stone crabs. They are one of the most delicate and one of the richest and one of the handsomest of all crustaceans. Little else is needed after eating some of these. It is very easy to overeat.

MENU: *Cold Florida stone crabs with mustard sauce*
        Tossed salad
        French bread
        Cold mangoes

COLD FLORIDA STONE CRABS WITH MUSTARD SAUCE:

Boil the claws about 20 minutes. Take a cloth folded in several thicknesses. Lay a hot claw on this cloth and crack each of the three sections with a wooden mallet or other strong instrument. Drain and chill. Arrange four claws on each plate. Serve with mustard sauce.

MUSTARD SAUCE:

To make mustard sauce, add to mayonnaise, preferably homemade in a blender and using lemon juice, one tablespoon of prepared French mustard. Serves 4.

CRAB MOUSSE

Velvety smooth and simple to prepare.

MENU: *Crab mousse, surrounded with hearts of artichokes and cherry tomatoes*
Hot biscuits
Blueberry tarts

CRAB MOUSSE:
2 tablespoons gelatin
1/4 cup diluted vinegar (1/2 water and 1/2 tarragon vinegar)
1 cup boiling clam or chicken broth
1 cup diced cucumbers
1 1/2 cups canned or frozen crab meat (carefully picked over)
1 teaspoon Worcestershire sauce
1 cup sour cream
1/2 small can water chestnuts, sliced
2 tablespoons capers

In the container of an electric blender put gelatin, vinegar, and clam or chicken broth. Cover and blend one minute. Add cucumber, crab meat and Worcestershire sauce. Blend one minute more. Remove from blender and stir in sour cream, water chestnuts and capers. Pour into a 1-quart mold and chill until firm. Unmold and serve on a bed of watercress. Serves 4.

CRAB SALAD

It seems a little cruel and tantalizing to say in several recipes, as I have, that you really should have lump crab meat, when it is available at a decent price only on certain sections of the Eastern seaboard. Crab salad can, of course, be made with canned or frozen crab meat.

MENU: *Sliced country ham*
Crab salad
Hot biscuits
Blackberry pie

CRAB SALAD:

1½ pounds lump or backfin crab meat, or 3 cans 6½
oz. crab meat, or 3 packages frozen king crab meat
½ cup chopped celery
¾ cup good mayonnaise
1 tablespoon capers
Garden lettuce
Yellow plum or cherry tomatoes

Remove any membranes from the crab meat, but do not pull it to pieces. Toss lightly with celery and mayonnaise. Chill. To serve, bed down on garden lettuce. Surround with tomatoes and sprinkle the top with capers. Serves 4–6.

CRAB AND ARTICHOKE SALAD

On the West Coast, where salads are especially glorious, because of their abundant and excellent fresh ingredients, they are usually served at the start of a meal. This one, which is a main dish salad, is one of the regional favorites.

MENU: *Crab and artichoke salad*
Popovers
Raspberry meringues

CBAB AND ARTICHOKE SALAD:
Lettuce wedges
½ cup sour cream
1 tablespoon finely minced chives
juice of ½ lemon
½ jar (6 ounce) of marinated artichoke hearts, cut in pieces and some of the marinade added to the sour cream
4 to 8 crab legs, depending on size, or 1 cup crab meat blended with the dressing

Arrange lettuce wedges on a platter. Mix sour cream, chives, lemon juice, and some of the marinade from the artichoke hearts. Arrange artichoke hearts decoratively around the lettuce wedges and add crab legs. Pour the dressing over all, or serve separately. If crab meat is used, blend with the dressing and pour over artichoke hearts. Serves 4.

AVOCADO WITH CRAB SALAD

Avocado halves and crab salad (or indeed shrimp or chicken salad) are a perfect combination, being delicate but surprisingly filling.

MENU: *Hot tomato with orange broth (heat equal amounts tomato juice and orange juice)*
Avocado with crab salad
Parker House rolls
Green gage plum pie

AVACADO WITH CRAB SALAD:

    2 ripe avocados, cut in half

    ½ pound lump crab meat, picked and membranes removed, or ½ pound cooked shrimp, peeled and deveined

    ¼ cup mayonnaise, preferably homemade

    2 tablespoons chopped celery

Mix crab meat with mayonnaise and celery and pile into avocado halves. Serves 4.

CRAB LOUIS

This is a classic West Coast salad, and, like lots of classics, there are many versions, each one absolutely the authentic one.

MENU: *Crab Louis*
        Garlic bread
        Honeydew melon with fresh blackberries

CRAB LOUIS:

    2 cans (6½-ounce) crab meat, or 2 frozen Dungeness crabs or 2 king crab legs or 2 packages frozen king crab meat

    ½ head lettuce, chopped fine

SAUCE:

    ¼ cup chopped mustard pickle

    ¼ cup catsup

    1 cup mayonnaise

    2 tablespoons finely chopped green onions

    2 tablespoons finely chopped green pepper

    2 tablespoons finely chopped green almonds

    ½ teaspoon Worcestershire sauce

Mix all sauce ingredients together. Pick over crab meat, removing any membranes. Mix with dressing and serve on chopped lettuce leaves. Serves 4 as a salad, more as an appetizer.

CRAB FEAST

This is not a dainty meal, nor one for the timid to cook. It is best eaten out of doors on rustic tables with plenty of paper napkins and with working facilities nearby. Some directions blandly assume that crabs are lying as quiet as oysters or clams while the preliminary preparations are going on. I speak with feeling, remembering some extra violent and aggressive crabs that got under the stove. I did win, finally. I was bigger.

MENU: *Maryland crab soup (p. 18)*
       Steamed crabs
       Watermelon
       Beer

STEAMED CRABS:
      Vinegar
      4 dozen live hard-shell or blue crabs
      Old Bay seafood seasoning
      Salt
      Butter

Take your largest cooking pot and place folded wire mesh, a trivet, or some other easily penetrable stand in it, so that the crabs will rest about 2 inches above the bottom of the pot. The crabs must be steamed and should not touch the boiling liquid below them. Mix 1 part vinegar to 2 parts water, enough to cover the bottom of the pot to a depth of about 1 inch. Bring this to a boil. To handle crabs, use kitchen tongs of some sort. The crab, understandably, is rather annoyed at this whole procedure and will fight back if given a chance. Pick up crabs one at a time with tongs. Check each one to make sure that it is still alive—there are quite often one or two fatalities per batch. Using a large spoon, sprinkle a generous amount of Old Bay seafood seasoning on the underside of each crab as you pick it up, then a generous amount of salt. This will irritate the crab and make it move violently, but deposit it firmly on the rack in the pot. Place as many crabs in the pot as it will hold letting the lid fit tightly. If you are using a smaller pot, you will have to steam them in several shifts. Use the same steaming mixture throughout, but add a little more water and vinegar if needed. Cover and then steam for 15 to 20 minutes. When done, place crabs on strips of paper toweling or newspaper to cool. Melt butter and pour one-half cup into small dishes, one for each person.

To eat the crabs, open the flap on the underside and use it as a lever to lift the top shell off. Remove all inside that is not covered by a thin shell. Break the crab in half and then, with a knife or by breaking, section the sides of the crab, one section to each leg. Remove surrounding shell to get white meat within. There are many different techniques for this. The claw meat is obtained by breaking the claw open with a wooden mallet. Dip meat in melted butter. Serves 8.

Three · LOBSTER AND ROCK LOBSTER

STIEFF'S ALMOST LOBSTER BISQUE

Fred Stieff, whose *Eat, Drink, and Be Merry in Maryland* published in 1932 is a highly personal compilation of traditional Maryland recipes, was wont to whip this up at the end of an impromptu evening while he stayed you with flagons of champagne. It is his version of a very well-known crab meat mixture.

MENU: *Stieff's almost lobster bisque*
Champagne
Pilot biscuit

STIEFF'S ALMOST LOBSTER BISQUE:
      1 can, 5oz., lobster
      1 can tomato paste
      1 can cream of pea soup
      1 pint light cream

Heat together and stir until blended and hot. Serve with pilot biscuits split and crisped in the oven. Serves 4.

BOILED LOBSTER

This is lobster *cooked the very best way,* so that "you can't escape the flavor," the distilled essence of the lobster, surely one of the best flavors in the world. For four people, it is better to buy four 1-pound lobsters and give each person a whole one, rather than give each person a piece of one. It is more dashing and dramatic. If lobster meat is to be used in another dish, of course, it is more economical to cook a couple of larger ones.

MENU: *Boiled lobster with melted butter*
Corn on the cob
Tossed green salad
Hot muffins
Vanilla ice cream with diced orange peel (stir in when soft and refreeze)
Lady fingers

BOILED LOBSTER:
4 1-pound lobsters
¼ cup butter

Lobsters must be well cleaned before cooking them this way. Turn on the faucet, grasping lobster at the back, and rinse the claws first, and then the body and back, bottom side first. Have a large kettle ready, containing one cup of boiling water. Put washed lobsters in kettle. Cover and turn the heat down one half. Cook 5 minutes, and then reduce the heat one half again. Cook 10 minutes more. Remove lobsters with tongs and let them cool. Serve warm, but not hot. Strain liquid from pan. From 4 lobsters there should be about 2 cups of juice. Melt butter in the juice and serve with the lobsters. If this is not being served elegantly, dunk hot muffins in the lobster juice. Serves 4.

BROILED LIVE LOBSTER

I, myself, am much too squeamish to split a live lobster which is not being at all passive during the process, but I can tell you ways to do it. Two methods take character of a kind that I don't have. First way, cross the large claws and hold firmly with the left hand. Plunge a sharp knife in at what seems to be the mouth and pull the knife quickly the length of the body and tail. Open the lobster and press flat. Second way, cut its spinal cord where the body and the tail meet, lay it on its back and split. Or best of all do as I do, and drop it into boiling water in your largest kettle (for soups, pastas or lobsters) for 3 minutes to kill it and then go on from there. Being the cautious type, I usually do the lobsters, one at a time. Put in together, they fight and try to crawl out, sometimes with just one cooked claw. Hold the lid down firmly during the first death throes.

MENU: *Broiled live lobster with melted butter*
 Sliced fresh tomatoes with vinaigrette dressing
 Grapefruit Alaska

BROILED LIVE LOBSTER:

 4 live lobsters, split (see instructions above)
 1½ cups cracker crumbs mixed with 1 tablespoon Worcestershire sauce and ½ teaspoon salt, or 1½ cups Colonna's flavored bread crumbs
 ⅓ cup melted butter (for the dressing)
 2 cups melted butter (½ cup per serving with lobster)

Remove dark veins, the sac near head and spongy tissue. Sometimes, this is difficult to identify. Save the greenish liver and the coral. These are both good to eat, and the knowing ones often spread them on a piece of French bread. Make a dressing of bread crumbs, seasoning and melted butter. Spread dressing generously in the cavity. Place on a greased broiler and broil 8 to 10 minutes, first on the split or meaty side and then on the other. Serve one lobster to each person with a half cup of melted butter.

BOILED LARGE LOBSTER (to have and to hold)

To my astonishment, when I was doing some of the last bit of writing on this book on Cape Cod, there were no instructions in the books for cooking a lobster over two pounds although the ones in the tank and the one we bought weighed six. The fishman told me. A lobster this size is tender and juicy. There are about 5½ cups of meat from a 6-pound lobster. That is usually enough for one main dish and a lobster cocktail for another meal or to fill avocado halves when mixed with chopped celery and mayonnaise. When cooked, it will keep several days or a week in the refrigerator. It will keep several weeks if frozen.

MENU: *Diced cooked lobster served hot with cold lemon butter*
Succotash
Bibb lettuce
Red plum halves and honeydew melon balls in white wine with curaçao

DICED COOKED LOBSTER SERVED WITH COLD LEMON BUTTER:
1 live lobster or 2 cups diced cooked meat
½ cup unsalted butter, softened to room temperature
2 tablespoons finely chopped fresh dill or fresh tarragon
2 tablespoons fresh lemon juice
Salt, pepper

Steam the lobster in 3 inches of water, covered, for 35 minutes.

Remove from water, slit the undershell with a knife or scissors and crack the claws. Remove dark vein, sac near the head, and spongy tissue. Save the greenish liver and coral. Dice the lobster meat. To make the butter, beat butter until fluffy. Add fresh chopped dill or tarragon, if available. If not, use chives or parsley. Add lemon juice, and cream some more. Chill before serving. Makes about ¾ cup of sauce.

LOBSTER STEW

There is something poetic about the wondrous flavor and simplicity of lobster stew, and one of the best recipes comes from the poet, Robert P. Tristram Coffin. He felt as strongly about the good foods from Maine as he did about poetry. This stew should be made of the very best ingredients, and the best, to him, were good Maine lobsters, milk, and cream. The flavors must be allowed to ripen in a cold place or refrigerator for 24 to 48 hours, before stew is reheated and served.

MENU: *Broiled water chestnuts wrapped in bacon*
Lobster stew
Dill pickles
Pilot crackers
Homemade doughnuts

LOBSTER STEW:
4 small-to-medium live lobsters
½ cup boiling sea water or ½ cup boiling water with a teaspoon of salt added
¼ pound slightly salted butter
2 cups milk, scalded
1 cup light coffee cream, scalded
Salt, pepper

Pick up lobsters from the back with tongs, or if you're really brave, with your hands. Some directions assume that lobsters just sit still waiting for you to pick them up. The fresh ones I have known do not stand still. They get loose, they run around the kitchen floor, and send poodles into hysterics. After lobsters are in the pot, cover and steam 10 minutes over a high heat. Let cool and shell. Remove meat as neatly as possible. Remove intestinal vein and lungs. Melt butter in a large pot and add the lobster meat, cut into pieces. Remove from heat and slowly add, while stirring constantly, the scalded milk and coffee cream. Add salt and pepper. Simmer for a few minutes, but do not boil. Remove from heat and cool 24 to 48 hours while the flavor is developing. Dr. Coffin did not believe in refrigeration, but he lived in Maine, where it is cool enough to keep this stew for two days without its spoiling. Further south, say from New York City on, I would prefer to keep this in the refrigerator. Reheat before serving and season to taste. Serves 4.

LOBSTER CANTONESE

This is perhaps the favorite dish to splurge on when eating in a Chinese restaurant.

MENU: *Lobster Cantonese*
       Rice
       Lemon sherbet

LOBSTER CANTONESE:

   ⅓ cup peanut oil, or more
   ¼ pound ground pork
   3-4 slices fresh ginger, minced
   1 tablespoon anchovy paste (or Dowsee fermented
      black soy beans)

1 cup chicken broth
2 cloves garlic
2 tablespoons cornstarch
2 live lobsters, 1 1/2 pounds each
3 eggs
2 green scallions, chopped
1 tablespoon Madras curry powder

Heat oil over low heat until smoking. There should be enough to cover the bottom of the skillet. Add ground pork and ginger and sauté until brown. Add anchovy paste or Dowsee, and chicken broth, garlic, curry powder and scallions. Meanwhile, split lobsters in half lengthwise then crosswise into one inch pieces. Remove the head, intestinal vein and stomach. Crack claws. Drop claws and pieces into mixture. Cook for 7-10 minutes, stirring occasionally. Add eggs and cornstarch mixed with water. Serve hot with rice. Serves 4.

CREAMED LOBSTER

One friend with exquisite taste in food, and who has eaten much fine food prepared superbly, insists that the very best way to eat lobster is creamed. She does, of course, mean the very best lobster and a cream sauce made with unsalted butter and real cream.

MENU: *Creamed lobster*
Peas
Tiny new potatoes
Leaf lettuce
Hot biscuits
Orange sherbet and madeleines

CREAMED LOBSTER:

    3 tablespoons butter
    3 tablespoons flour
    1½ cup light or heavy cream
    Salt, white pepper
    1 egg yolk, beaten
    2 cups diced cooked lobster

Melt butter and add flour. Stir until almost dry. Add cream a little at a time, stirring constantly until smooth and thickened. Add salt and white pepper. Remove from heat and stir in one beaten egg yolk. Add lobster meat. Serves 4.

LOBSTER NEWBURG

The dish so dear to the hearts of the Victorians. They served it with dash in chafing dishes at after-theater parties.

MENU: *Lobster Newburg*
       Bibb lettuce salad
       Hot rolls
       Coffee mousse

LOBSTER NEWBURG:

    2 cups diced cooked lobster
    4 tablespoons butter
    ½ teaspoon paprika
    ⅓ cup sherry
    1 tablespoon flour
    1 cup heavy cream
    2 egg yolks, beaten
    Salt, white pepper

Heat lobster in three tablespoons of butter with the sherry

and paprika. While this is being done, melt the rest of the butter in the top of a double boiler. Add flour, cook a minute or two until almost dry, then add cream, stirring constantly until smooth and thickened. Stir one mixing spoon of hot cream sauce into beaten egg yolks and stir until thoroughly blended. Add this to the rest of mixture in the double boiler and stir until well blended. Add lobster, salt and pepper. Stir, and serve on toast. This may be done in a chafing dish if you like to perform before an audience. Serves 4.

LOBSTER CURRY

Curries can be very simple like this one or very complicated. Made either way, the flavor is better if the dish is permitted to ripen in the refrigerator before heating and serving.

MENU: *Lobster curry*
Rice
Chutney, almonds
Fresh raspberries and cream

LOBSTER CURRY:
3 tablespoons butter or oil
2 medium onions, chopped
1 fat clove garlic, chopped
1 tablespoon Madras curry powder, or more to taste
Juice of 1 lemon
1 tablespoon grated lemon peel
1 cup evaporated milk
Salt
1 pound lobster meat, pulled apart

Sauté onion and garlic in butter or oil until pale yellow. Add curry powder, blending in well, then add the lemon juice and peel. Cook and stir until smooth, add evaporated milk, stirring until smooth again. Add lobster. Either heat and serve or let stand in the sauce overnight to "ripen," then heat over very low heat for 45 minutes to an hour. Serves 4.

LOBSTER CASSEROLE

Gracefully impromptu.

MENU: *Lobster casserole*
Watercress, endive, grapefruit, hearts of palm salad
with French dressing

LOBSTER CASSEROLE:

3 cans (5½-ounce) lobster, cubed
1 can frozen condensed cream of shrimp soup
½ cup light cream
¼ cup sherry
¼ cup slivered almonds
1 can cooked wild rice
Salt, pepper

Combine all the ingredients in a buttered casserole. Heat in a 350° oven until hot (20 to 25 minutes). Serves 4.

LOBSTER THERMIDOR

Lobster itself is festive, but this recipe makes it still more a dish of ceremony. As with many classic dishes there are many versions. These are the ingredients, if not the exact proportions, used in this dish as served at Lapérouse in Paris.

MENU: *Lobster thermidor*
Hot artichokes with melted butter
Salt sticks
Wine sherbet

LOBSTER THERMIDOR:
2 broiled lobsters, 1½ pounds each, (p. 43)
3 tablespoons butter
3 tablespoons flour
1½ cups light cream
1 tablespoon prepared mustard
2 tablespoons finely chopped chives
Coral from lobsters
Grated Swiss Gruyère or Emmenthaler cheese

Remove lobster meat from shells and cut into bite-size pieces. Wash the shells well, and dry. Sauté lobster in the butter briefly; then add flour, cream, mustard. Stir well until smooth and thickened. Do not boil. Add salt and pepper to taste, chives, and coral of the lobster. Spoon into 4 cleaned halves of lobster shells. Sprinkle the tops with grated cheese. Brown under broiler or in a 450° oven for about 10 minutes. Serves 4.

LOBSTER MARYLAND

Which is to say, lobster prepared somewhat in the fashion of terrapin à la Maryland and the ingredients are much easier to come by.

MENU: *Lobster Maryland*
Fresh asparagus
Spoonbread
Watercress and tomato salad
Lemon soufflé

LOBSTER MARYLAND:

> 2 cups cooked lobster, diced
> 4 tablespoons butter
> 1 cup heavy cream
> 2 egg yolks, hard cooked and crushed
> 1 tablespoon tomato paste
> White pepper
> Pinch of cayenne
> 3 tablespoons sherry

Sauté lobster lightly in the butter. Add cream and heat but do not let this boil. Remove from the heat, let cool slightly before adding crushed hard-cooked egg yolks. Stir until thickened. Add tomato paste, white pepper to taste, and a pinch of cayenne (which most fine professional chefs find essential to many seafood dishes). Stir in sherry and serve on toast points or on spoonbread. Serves 4.

LOBSTER SOUFFLE

Traditional lobster soufflé, which this is, is different from the usual soufflé that is baked in a straight-sided dish. It is a little more trouble to prepare but much, much more dramatic a presentation.

MENU: *Lobster soufflé*
Risi pisi
Watercress and sliced water chestnuts

LOBSTER SOUFFLÉ:

> 2 boiled lobsters (1¼ pounds apiece) slit in half
> 3 tablespoons butter
> 3 tablespoons flour
> 1 cup light cream

2 tablespoons sherry
3 eggs, separated
Salt, pepper
Bread crumbs

Remove meat from the shells and dice. Clean out the shells and butter them. Melt butter, add flour and cook until almost dry. Add cream a little at a time, stirring until smooth and thickened. Add sherry, seasoning, egg yolks, and the diced lobster. Whip egg whites until stiff and fold into the lobster mixture. Pile lightly into cleaned and buttered lobster half shells. Sprinkle tops with bread crumbs. Place in oven preheated to 350° and bake 15-20 minutes. Serve immediately. Serves 4.

LOBSTER FRA DIAVOLO

Traditionally this dish is made with lobster, but the sauce is fine with lobster tails, too. Usually the sauce is made first, and then the lobster (plunged in boiling water for 3 minutes first to kill it) is either split and baked with the sauce poured over it, or cut in pieces, shells and all, and cooked in the sauce. If lobster tails are used, cut away the shell on flat side of the tail and remove the dark vein.

MENU: *Lobster fra diavolo*
Noodles with butter and poppy seeds
Marinated artichoke hearts
Melon balls in white wine with blueberries

LOBSTER FRA DIAVOLO:
⅓ cup olive oil
2 cloves garlic, diced
⅛ teaspoon crushed red pepper
1 teaspoon salt

1 tablespoon chopped parsley
1 tablespoon vinegar
1 tablespoon prepared mustard
2 picnic size (10½-ounce) cans tomato purée
2 lobsters, 1½ pounds each, or 4 lobster tails

Cook garlic in hot olive oil until slightly browned. Add red pepper, salt, parsley, vinegar, mustard, and tomato purée. Simmer for 30 minutes. Prepare lobsters as directed above or lobster tails. Arrange in a baking dish and spoon tomato sauce over the flesh side of the lobster or lobster tails. Bake in an oven preheated to 350° about 25 minutes for the lobster tails, 35 minutes for the lobster halves. Serves 4.

LOBSTER SALAD

Elegant and Victorian.

MENU: *Hot mushroom broth*
Lobster salad
Hot butterflake rolls
Key lime pie

LOBSTER SALAD:

3 cups diced cooked lobster or lobster tails
1 cup diced celery root (may be bought pickled and drained) or 1 cup diced fresh celery
½ cup French dressing
Mayonnaise
Greens

Toss diced lobster and celery or celery root lightly with French dressing. Marinate in the refrigerator 2 or 3 hours. Just before serving mix with enough mayonnaise to hold and arrange on a bed of greens. Serves 4.

LOBSTER ROLLS

Among the delights found when traveling and eating in Maine are lobster rolls. Some are made with hamburger rolls, but I prefer to use the brown-and-serve hard rolls, split and spread with melted butter.

MENU: *Lobster rolls*
Blueberry pie

LOBSTER ROLLS:
6 brown-and-serve club rolls or 6 hard rolls
Butter
Lobster salad (p. 54)

Heat or brown the rolls, split and butter. Pile lobster salad lavishly inside and serve. Serves 3 to 6 depending on appetites.

LOBSTER MOUSSE

Lobster mousse is an elegant dish that lifts the spirits on a hot day and soothes jangled nerves. It does not, however, fit in with any low calorie, low cholesterol regime.

MENU: *Lobster mousse with sliced cucumbers, white grapes and watercress*
Hot butterflake rolls
Honeydew melon with pineapple chunks, fresh black-berries

LOBSTER MOUSSE:
1 envelope unflavored gelatin
1 tablespoon tarragon vinegar
⅔ cup boiling water

> 2 or 3 drops red coloring (more looks garish, none is
>   too anemic)
> 1 cucumber, peeled and diced
> ½ cup mayonnaise
> ½ cup heavy cream
> 2 cups lobster meat, fresh, frozen or canned
> Sliced cucumbers
> White grapes
> Watercress

Put gelatin, tarragon vinegar and boiling water in the container of an electric blender. Blend a few seconds. Add red coloring, cucumber, mayonnaise and cream and blend 30 seconds. Add lobster and blend for a minute or more. This may be made without a blender. If so, soak the gelatin in terragon vinegar and 2 tablespoons of cold water. Dissolve in boiling water, add red coloring, the cucumber, which should be chopped very fine, mayonnaise and the cream, stiffly beaten. Fold in finely chopped lobster. Either way, turn into a quart mold and chill until firm. Unmold on a bed of watercress and arrange cucumber slices in overlapping design around the mold. Sprinkle with white grapes. Serves 4.

BOILED LOBSTER TAILS

Frozen lobster tails are indeed not so tender as Maine lobsters, but they have some very special assets. For one thing, they are frozen and do not fight back at you. Another, they are neat and tidy, easy to use and keep on hand in the freezer, and reasonably inexpensive. The meat is likely to seem more tender when it is sliced before serving.

MENU: *Boiled lobster tails with butter and tarragon vinegar*
Lima beans
Tiny new potatoes, boiled in their skins
Lemon pudding cake

BOILED LOBSTER TAILS:
4 lobster tails
Salt
Bay leaf
¼ cup white wine
1 small onion, chopped
Pinch of cayenne pepper

Put lobster tails in a saucepan, cover with boiling water and add salt, bay leaf, white wine, onions and cayenne pepper. Cover and bring to a boil. Cook 15 minutes for small, 17 minutes for large tails. Serves 4.

BROILED LOBSTER TAILS

I am a little squeamish about cutting up a live lobster so I eat them in sea-food restaurants. At home I broil nicely dead and immobile lobster tails. They have a good nutty flavor and character of their own.

MENU: *Broiled lobster tails*
French fried potatoes
Mashed yellow squash
Sesame seed rolls
Pears, stewed in wine

BROILED LOBSTER TAILS:
> 4 large lobster tails or 8 small ones (they are more
>   tender)
> Butter
> Salt, pepper
> Lemon quarters

Split undershell lengthwise and nick the curved shell in several places to prevent curling. Pour melted butter on the meat in the split shells lavishly and put under broiler preheated to 450°. Broil 10-15 minutes or until meat is golden brown and slightly charred around the edges. Serve with lemon quarters. Serves 4.

BROILED STUFFED LOBSTER TAILS

A modest version of a truly superb dish.

MENU: *Broiled stuffed lobster tails*
> *Tossed green salad*
> *Fresh fruit*

BROILED STUFFED LOBSTER TAILS:
> 8 frozen lobster tails (about 8 ounces each)
> 1/3 cup butter
> 1 tablespoon finely chopped green onion
> 1/3 cup flour
> 1 teaspoon salt
> Pinch of cayenne pepper
> 2 cups half-and-half (half milk, half cream)
> 1 pound or 2 cans, 6½ oz., crab meat
> ¾ cup soft buttered bread crumbs

Split the undershell of lobster tails and nick in several places to prevent curling. Remove meat from shell and cut in bite-sized pieces. Melt butter and sauté onion briefly; stir in flour, salt and cayenne. Cook for a minute or two until it becomes dry. Add the half-and-half a little at a time until it is smooth and thickened. Add crab meat which has been picked over to remove membrane. Add lobster meat. Pile mixture into shells. Sprinkle with buttered crumbs. Broil or bake for 20-25 minutes in 450° oven. Serves 4.

CRAYFISH

There are times of the year, I am told, when all Scandinavians go out of their minds. It is crayfish time. Crayfish are smaller and more delicate than lobsters but resemble them quite a lot. They are cooked in large amounts, served in pyramids, and eaten with butter and dill. There are places here where one can get crayfish and possibly the mania overtakes one automatically.

MENU: *Crayfish with butter and dill*
Broiled liver with bacon
Broccoli
Cheese sticks
Walnut spice cake

CRAYFISH:
COURT BOUILLON:
1 stalk celery with leaves, chopped
4 sprigs parsley
½ bay leaf
1 cup white wine
1 small onion, cut in pieces
2 quarts water

      1 tablespoon cracked black pepper
    40 live crayfish
    Dill butter

Simmer ingredients for court bouillon for 20 minutes. Meanwhile clean crayfish, removing the dark vein. Plunge crayfish into boiling court bouillon and cook for 10 minutes. Drain and serve with melted butter and minced dill. Serves 4 Americans, much fewer Scandinavians.

Four · MUSSELS

MUSSEL BARQUETTES

A pleasant change from most hot canapés and simple to make when tiny puff shells are bought ready-made.

MENU: *Mussel barquettes*
Chicken broiled with butter and lemon
Rice
Mixed green salad
Pound cake with lemon sherbet and chocolate sauce

MUSSEL BARQUETTES:
Tiny puff shells
Fresh steamed mussels or canned mussels, drained
2 tablespoons butter
2 tablespoons flour
1 cup light cream
1 egg yolk, beaten
Salt, pepper

Melt butter and mix with flour; cook until dry. Add cream and cook over low heat, stirring until smooth and thickened. Remove from fire. Add beaten egg yolk, salt and pepper. Return to fire for a minute or two. Put a mussel into each tiny puff shell. Add a spoonful of sauce. Bake in an oven preheated to 450° for 5 minutes or until browned. Serve hot.

MEDIA DOLMA

The Greeks stuff all sorts of edibles—squash, peppers, eggplants, melons, grape leaves, and so on. One of my favorite appetizers is this traditional Greek way of serving stuffed mussels.

MENU: *Media dolma*
Lamb, tomato and okra stew
Dandelion salad with sliced, hard-cooked eggs
Pideh (flat Armenian bread)
Pear and custard pie

MEDIA DOLMA:
½ cup raw rice
¼ cup olive oil
1 chopped onion
1 cup consommé (or water)
1 teaspoon allspice
Salt, pepper
¼ cup pine nuts or pignolias
2 tablespoons dried currants
2 dozen mussels

Cook rice in oil with chopped onion until golden. Add consommé or water, allspice, salt, pepper, pine nuts and currants. Bring to a boil, cover, turn heat down and simmer over very low heat for 15 to 20 minutes or until rice is tender and liquid absorbed. Meanwhile, scrub mussels very carefully until the shells are smooth and gleaming. Put in water, bring to boil, and simmer until shells open. Remove and drain reserving liquid. Take off top shell and cover each mussel in its shell with rice stuffing, pressing down. Put in a shallow casserole with 2 cups of water, using the liquid in which the mussels were cooked. Cover and bake in a 325° oven 45 minutes or over low heat on top of stove until the water evaporates. Serves 4.

STUFFED MUSSELS

A lusty version from around the Mediterranean, quite different from the delicate Greek Media Dolma and for a different day and different mood and a different menu.

MENU: *Stuffed mussels*
Capellini (very fine pasta) dressed with garlic-flavored olive oil and sprinkled with coarsely chopped walnuts
Baked tomatoes
Italian bread
Ricotta pie

STUFFED MUSSELS:
1 head lettuce
1 small onion, chopped
1 clove garlic, minced
⅓ cup finely chopped parsley
⅓ cup chopped salami
18 mussels, scrubbed, the beards removed and opened on their shells
2 cans tomato sauce
1 cup white wine

Steam lettuce in a little water for about ten minutes. Drain and chop fine. Mix with onion, garlic, parsley and salami. Put a spoonful on each mussel in its shell, tie tightly with string. Cook slowly in sauce and wine for about 20 minutes. Remove strings and serve in sauce. There is no salt or pepper needed with the mussels; they and the salami have enough. Serve 4 to each of four and the other 2 to the hungriest.

MUSSELS IN ANCHOVY SAUCE

Italians, who treat all sea food with care and imagination, cook mussels with this positive seasoning, and serve them cold.

MENU: *Mussels in anchovy sauce*
Veal scallopine with mushrooms and marsala
Risi pisi
Tossed green salad
Pears with cheese

MUSSELS IN ANCHOVY SAUCE:

½ cup olive oil
1 clove garlic
8 anchovy fillets, chopped
4 dozen mussels, scrubbed, opened and removed from the shells
1 cup dry white wine
1 cup wine vinegar
⅓ cup finely chopped parsley
Freshly ground black pepper

Sauté garlic in oil in a large deep skillet until golden but *not* browned. Discard garlic. Add anchovies and mussels. Cover and cook over medium heat 5 to 6 minutes. Add wine and vinegar and cook for about 5 to 7 minutes uncovered, or until liquid has been reduced by more than half. Put in a bowl, sprinkle with parsley and pepper. Let cool, then chill in refrigerator for a day or more. Serve mussels chilled as an appetizer, with the drained sauce on the side. Serves 4.

MUSSELS WITH SNAIL BUTTER

Mussels are a specialty in Belgium and *moules* prepared this way are found in most restaurants. This appetizer may be done a day ahead and kept ready to pop in the oven at the last minute. The mussels are served in their shells.

MENU: *Mussels with snail butter*
Roast leg of lamb
Eggplant soufflé
French bread
Orange sections with banana liqueur

MUSSELS WITH SNAIL BUTTER:
3 pounds mussels, washed and scrubbed well
1 cup court bouillon (see p. 59)
4 slices bacon
1 clove garlic, cut in half
Snail butter (p. 191)

Steam well-scrubbed mussels in court bouillon with the bacon and garlic until they are open. Remove from liquid and pull off one shell. Spread some snail butter on each mussel in its shell. Either bake immediately at 350° for 5 minutes or cover with Pliofilm and keep in refrigerator until wanted. Bake at 350° for 10 minutes if taken directly from the refrigerator. Serves 4-6.

COLD MUSSELS IN MUSTARD SAUCE

Mussels are too little known in this country although we have many growing here. Before gathering them fresh, check with the Sanitation Department to see whether the waters around are polluted or not. There are still plenty of mussels in waters that are not. They are neat to serve in their own shells with, perhaps, some small bamboo or ivory forks sold inexpensively in Japanese stores.

MENU: *Cold mussels in mustard sauce*
Broiled chicken breasts basted with butter, lemon
juice and Tabasco
Lima beans
Potato and chive soufflé
Wine sherbet

COLD MUSSELS IN MUSTARD SAUCE:
2 dozen mussels, well scrubbed and beards removed
½ cup white wine
1 teaspoon chopped onion
¼ cup mayonnaise
¼ cup Gulden's mustard
Tray of crushed ice

Steam mussels in white wine with onion for about 5 minutes or until they open. Remove and tear off top shell. Let cool. Mix mayonnaise with mustard and spoon over the mussels, adding more, mixed in the same half-and-half proportions, if needed. Chill for several hours. Serve dramatically on a tray of crushed ice, if possible, with small forks on the side. They may be served on a tray without ice if less fuss is desired. Serves 4 or more if there are other first courses.

BILLI BI SOUP

This is one of the truly sublime soups, almost a soup to dream of. In Europe, mussels are called the poor man's oysters, but this soup is for grand occasions or perhaps a time when you just want to feel grand. It was created and named for William B. Leeds by Maxim's.

MENU: *Billi Bi Soup*
Broiled lobster
Mushroom risotta
French bread
Marinated hearts of artichokes
Fresh raspberries with macaroons

BILLI BI SOUP:

2 pounds mussels
4 tablespoons chopped onions
3 tablespoons chopped shallots
2 cups heavy cream
1 cup dry white wine
Salt, pepper
Pinch of cayenne

Scrub mussels well with a wire brush or copper scouring pad, and remove beards. Put in a large kettle with onion, shallots, seasonings and wine. Cover and bring to a boil. Simmer 5 to 10 minutes until the mussels have opened. Remove from heat and take the shells and the whole mussels from liquid. Discard any unopened mussels. Strain liquid through a sieve lined with cheesecloth. Heat with the cream, but do not let boil. Serve either hot or cold from a tureen and garnish with a few mussels. Save the rest of the mussels for another dish, say media dolma. Serves 4 blissfully.

MUSSELS A LA MARINIERE

For this dish, the most important thing is to scrub the mussels until they gleam like black opals. That means using a wire brush, the kind used for suede, and also using your fingernails. Allow plenty of time for this. It's a beautiful dish.

MENU: *Mussels à la Marinière*
Watercress and tomato aspic with hearts of artichoke imbedded in it and a dressing of half sour cream and half mayonnaise
Lots of French bread for dunking
Apricot tarts

MUSSELS A LA MARINIERE:

3 pounds mussels, scrubbed clean, in fact almost manicured
2 tablespoons chopped parsley
1 medium-sized onion, minced
¼ teaspoon rosemary
⅓ cup olive oil
1 cup dry white wine
Salt, pepper

Brown onion, parsley, and rosemary in olive oil. Transfer to large deep individual casseroles with covers, dividing into four parts. Add mussels in their shells, then the wine, salt, and pepper. Cover tightly and bake in a medium oven for about 15 minutes, or until the mussels open and are a pretty orange. Tear off top shells, but leave the others in the juices. Use shells for scooping up liquid; an oyster fork is usual for the mussels. Mop up the rest of liquid with French bread. Serves 4.

MUSSELS STUFFED AND BAKED IN THE TOULOUSE MANNER

While this is called the Toulouse manner, and is, it does sound as if it were the taking-off point for Mr. Alciatore's Oysters Rockefeller.

MENU: *Mussels stuffed and baked in the Toulouse manner*
Broiled tomato halves
French fried onions
French fried potatoes
Pineapple cheesecake

MUSSELS STUFFED AND BAKED IN THE TOULOUSE MANNER:
2 dozen mussels, scrubbed and steamed open
3 tablespoons oil
1 clove garlic, minced
1 onion, chopped
1 cup chopped cooked spinach
Fresh bread crumbs
Freshly grated Parmesan cheese
More oil

Arrange mussels on the half shell in four pie tins half-filled with rock salt or on a cookie sheet. Sauté garlic and onion in oil until lightly browned. Add spinach and stir to blend. Spread on mussels. Sprinkle with bread crumbs, then with cheese, and then with oil. Bake in an oven preheated to 350° until lightly browned. Serves 4.

FRIED MUSSELS WITH SKORDALIA

One long-time admirer of all things Greek—food, people, architecture and beautiful luminous light—feels that one of his most triumphant gastronomic discoveries in Greece was fried mussels. He uses them as a symbol of the kind of things the Greeks do with their food that the French don't, but actually they fry mussels in very much the same way. They are, indeed, good.

MENU: *Fried mussels with skordalia (a variant of garlic mayonnaise with ground nuts)*
Rice pilaff
Cooked okra, marinated in French dressing
Pideh
Grapefruit Alaska

FRIED MUSSELS:
2 dozen mussels or 2 cans mussels, drained
Oil for frying

FRITTER BATTER:
1½ cups all-purpose flour
1 teaspoon salt
1 tablespoon melted butter or cooking oil
2 egg yolks, slightly beaten
¾ cup beer, opened long enough to lose its effervescence
2 egg whites, stiffly beaten

Put all batter ingredients except egg whites in an electric blender. Blend 10 to 20 seconds, then let stand in the refrigerator at least 2 hours, preferably 10 to 12.

Scrub mussels and steam until they just open. Remove from shells, let cool and dry thoroughly before dipping in fritter batter into which egg whites have been folded. Cook as many at a time as the frying basket will hold without crowding, in oil heated to 375°. The mussels should take 3 to 5 minutes to brown. Drain on paper towels. Serve hot with cold skordalia. Serves 4.

SKORDALIA: (This can be bought at a Greek food store, but it has a considerably greater amount of garlic.)
2 cloves garlic, peeled and chopped
1 slice of bread, without the crust
2 tablespoons filberts, walnuts or almonds, ground fine
2 tablespoons vinegar
1 1/2 cups mayonnaise
Pinch of salt

Mash garlic in a mortar with a pestle. Add the slice of bread, which has been soaked in water and squeezed to remove excess liquid. Mix together with a spoon and add ground nuts, stirring until it makes a paste. Add vinegar a little at a time. The consistency should be that of mayonnaise. A simpler version of this can be made by adding to mayonnaise, preferably made in a blender, 1/2 cup of blanched almonds, 2 cloves of garlic, and 2 tablespoons of parsley clusters. Blend for 15 seconds. Makes 1 1/2 cups.

MUSSEL AND RICE PILAFF

Those unfortunate enough not to live near the fresh mussel region may buy them in cans. In this recipe either fresh steamed mussels or canned ones may be used.

MENU: *Mussel and rice pilaff*
Orange and onion slices on watercress
French bread
Whole fresh peeled peaches in a pitcher of white wine

MUSSEL AND RICE PILAFF:

>   3 tablespoons olive oil
>   1 cup raw rice
>   ½ red or green sweet pepper, chopped
>   2 cups chicken broth
>   1 hot Spanish sausage (chorizo), cut in pieces
>   2 pounds fresh mussels, steamed and removed from
>   shells, or 2 cans mussels, drained
>   ½ pound shrimp, peeled and deveined, or canned
>   shrimp, rinsed and drained
>   Paprika
>   Pepper

Cook pepper and rice in olive oil until pepper is limp and rice opaque, but not browned. Add chicken broth and sausage. Bring to a boil. Cover and turn the heat very low and cook 20 minutes. Add steamed mussels removed from shells, or canned ones drained, and the shrimp, paprika and pepper. Stir around, cover and cook over very low heat about 5 minutes. Serve immediately. Serves 4.

SMOKED MUSSEL PUDDING

See Smoked Oyster Pudding. Follow recipe, using smoked mussels in place of oysters.

Five · OYSTERS

MUSHROOM CAPS WITH OYSTERS

A dainty and dramatic way of serving oysters as an hors d'oeuvre.

MENU: *Mushroom caps with oysters   Drinks*
Hot cheese balls
Raw vegetables with sour cream dip

MUSHROOM CAPS WITH OYSTERS:
Large mushroom caps
Melted butter
Oysters
Finely chopped chives

Brush mushroom caps inside and out with melted butter. (Use the stems, chopped, in another dish another time.) Place a plump oyster on each mushroom cap. Arrange on a cookie sheet or pie tin. Bake in an oven preheated to 400° until the mushrooms are lightly cooked and the edges of the oysters curl. Serve warm.

SMOKED OYSTER DIP

This is a nice change from the ubiquitous clam dip and onion dip, good as they both are.

MENU: *Smoked oyster dip with triscuit*
Broiled steaks
Broccoli with Hollandaise
Baked potatoes
Watercress
French bread
Raspberry sherbet with crisp chocolate cookies

SMOKED OYSTER DIP:

1 package (8 ounce) cream cheese, softened at room temperature
2 tablespoons sherry
1 teaspoon grated onion
1 teaspoon paprika
1 tablespoon finely chopped chives
1 jar smoked oysters, chopped

Mix together and chill long enough to let the flavors mix well, but serve at room temperature. Makes about a cup and a quarter of dip. Serve with Triscuit.

ANGELS ON HORSEBACK OR PIGS IN BLANKETS

Angels on horseback is the English term, and pigs in blankets is the American, but neither seems to be a very apt description of an oyster wrapped in bacon and broiled. They are very good whether served with cocktails here or as a savory in England at the end of the meal, after dessert.

MENU: *Angels on horseback or pigs in blankets*
Pork loin with sour cherry sauce
Lima beans
Baked sweet potatoes
Chicory with Russian dressing
Orange custard

ANGELS ON HORSEBACK OR PIGS IN BLANKETS:

Take large oysters and simmer in their juice until the edges just curl, or use them raw. Drain and wrap each one in a thin piece of bacon and fasten with a toothpick. Broil until the bacon is crisp. Serve on toast.

RAW OYSTERS

I do not like to frustrate people who live inland or make them unhappy, but most of the time I think that the only way, absolutely the only way at all, to taste oysters at their blissful best is to eat them raw from the half shell. To do this you must be very near the regions where they are gathered. It is best to eat them on your own terrace, shucking them as you go, and eating them straight, with no fussy sauces or anything except, perhaps, some good, cold beer. Even experienced whiskey drinkers refrain while eating oysters. For some chemical reason, they become leathery and indigestible.

It is true that there is a special knack to opening oysters and it also requires some strength. If you look at professional oyster openers, their fingers always have quite a few cuts. On the other hand, you want the best, don't you? And oysters that come in cardboard containers already opened are not the same. To open you need first, in addition to the oysters, an oyster knife which can be bought along the Atlantic seaboard for about 35 cents. Take an oyster in your left hand with curved side down, then take the oyster knife in your right hand and work along the edge of the shell until you find a place where the knife can be inserted. Work the knife around a bit, and once you have loosened the shell, lift the top off. Loosen the oyster from the top if necessary. Smooth the oyster around on the bottom shell with the knife. It may be necessary, if you cannot find a place where you can easily insert the blade to tap at the edges with the knife or the handle in order to chip a place open. Once the oyster is opened, if you are being informal and a real pro, and sitting on the outside steps, you slurp it off the shell. If you are being more formal and dainty, you of course use an oyster fork. Somehow, if you serve raw oysters on plates at the table, you do not get enough. Perhaps because it seems rather greedy to eat plate after plate, but not greedy to eat them by the dozens, one by one, as they are handed to you by the oyster opener. However, I am not against sitting down to a proper meal at a proper table, *after* I have had my fill of oysters.

MENU: *Raw oysters*
Roast beef
Yorkshire pudding
Cooked green beans with Roquefort dressing
Deep-dish apple pie with whipped cream and bits of crystallized ginger

DEVILED OYSTERS

These can be deviled on their own half shells or baked in baking shells that can be bought in most places carrying cooking equipment.

MENU: *Deviled oysters*
Italian green beans
Rice cooked in clam broth with diced, seeded tomato
Onion rolls
Kugelhopf

DEVILED OYSTERS:
2 dozen raw oysters
3 tablespoons butter
3 tablespoons flour
1 cup chicken broth
Pinch nutmeg
1 to 3 teaspoons prepared mustard
Salt, pepper
1 cup fresh bread crumbs
2 tablespoons butter
2 tablespoons lemon juice

Simmer oysters in their own juice until edges curl. Drain and arrange on half shells which you have washed and dried, or on baking shells. Put shells on a cookie sheet. Meanwhile make a sauce by melting the butter and cooking with well-blended flour until slightly dried. Add chicken broth, a little at a time, stirring until smooth and thickened. Add nutmeg, mustard, salt and pepper. Spread sauce over oysters. Sprinkle with bread crumbs and dot with butter. Bake in an oven preheated to 350° until lightly browned. Reduce butter and lemon juice to about half. Serve with the oysters. Serves 4 to 6.

GOLDEN DOOR BAKED OYSTERS

The Golden Door Restaurant at Kennedy Airport serves fine food with a fine presentation.

MENU: *Golden Door baked oysters*
Roast beef
Watercress and endive salad
French bread
Pears and cheese

GOLDEN DOOR BAKED OYSTERS:
2 tablespoons butter
2 tablespoons flour
1 cup half-and-half
2 tablespoons sherry
Pinch of mace
Salt, pepper
1 can (6½ oz.) crab meat, drained and pulled apart
2 dozen oysters on the half shell
4 pie tins or baking dishes half filled with rock salt.

Melt butter, add flour and stir and cook until half dry. Add the half-and-half or milk a bit at a time until sauce is smooth and thickened. Add sherry, salt, pepper and mace. Stir in crab meat and spread a spoonful of the mixture over each oyster. Heat the pans of rock salt in an oven preheated to 450°. Remove from oven and arrange 6 oysters spread with crab meat mixture in their shells on the hot salt. Return to hot oven for 3-5 minutes or just until the mixture gets hot and bubbly. Serve piping hot. Serves 4.

BAKED OYSTERS WITH WINE AND WALNUTS

A quite different version of baked oysters.

MENU: *Baked oysters with wine and walnuts*
Potato soufflé

Mixed green salad
Hard rolls
Dried apricots in lemon jelly

BAKED OYSTERS WITH WINE AND WALNUTS:
  ¼ cup butter
  1 clove garlic, minced
  2 shallots, minced
  2 anchovies, minced
  ⅓ cup chopped walnuts
  1 tablespoon chopped parsley
  3 tablespoons dry white wine
  2 dozen raw oysters, on the half shell
  3 strips bacon, cooked and crumbled

Sauté garlic, shallots and anchovies in butter. Add walnuts, parsley and white wine. Mix well. Spread on oysters on the half shell. Top with crumbled cooked bacon. Bake on pie tins half filled with rock salt in a 350° oven for 10 minutes or more. Serves 4.

OYSTER STEW

All of the oyster stews found along the Eastern Coast, around the Chesapeake, are much the same in their basic ingredients. Only the proportions change. Some have more oysters per bowl and some have more cream. Six to a bowl is the minimum amount of oysters, and eight to ten about right. The most I have ever seen and eaten was eighteen small oysters in one large bowl. That was an epic occasion. The Pennsylvania Dutch always break pretzels in their stew, which seems odd but preferable to more innocuous oyster crackers. I am a purist about oyster stew and do not like any seasoning except paprika.

MENU: *Oyster stew with pretzels*
Fried chicken
Cole slaw with cream dressing
Hot rolls
Cherry pie

OYSTER STEW:
1 quart oysters
1 quart of milk or half milk and half cream
4 tablespoons butter
Paprika

Heat oysters in their juices until the edges curl. At the same
time heat the milk, or half milk and half cream, almost to the
boil, but remove from the heat just before that point. Pour
the two together off the fire and pour into four warm deep
soup bowls, allotting the oysters more or less evenly. Put 1
tablespoon of butter in each bowl and sprinkle the top with
paprika. Serves 4.

OYSTER BISQUE

This is the most subtle and elegant of oyster soups.

MENU: *Oyster bisque*
Broiled steaks
Broiled mushrooms
Baked tomatoes, stuffed with bread cubes and
anchovies
Onion rolls
Coffee ice cream with hot fudge sauce

OYSTER BISQUE:
>1 slice onion
>1 stalk celery, diced
>2 tablespoons butter
>1 quart oysters and juice
>2 cups light cream
>Salt, white pepper
>Dash of Tabasco

Cook onion and celery in butter until translucent, but do not brown. Put in an electric blender with half the oysters and juice. Blend 10 to 15 seconds. Add the rest of the oysters and blend 10 seconds more. Put in an enameled saucepan with cream, salt, pepper and Tabasco and simmer over a low heat, stirring constantly. Do not allow to come to a boil. Serves 4 to 6.

OYSTERS, PHILADELPHIA STYLE

Simple, savory and delicious.

MENU: *Oysters, Philadelphia style*
>*Creamed spinach*
>*Parsley new potatoes*
>*Sliced cucumbers with French dressing*
>*Hot toast*
>*Vanilla ice cream softened and mixed with diced*
>*orange peel and curaçao*

OYSTERS, PHILADELPHIA STYLE:
>3 tablespoons butter
>2 dozen raw oysters and their juice
>Salt, white pepper
>Thin slices toast

Simmer the oysters in butter and their own juices until edges curl. Add salt to taste and white pepper. Serve poured over the toast in a shallow casserole. Serves 4.

WILLIE'S CURRIED OYSTERS

Ben Gunn, the seaman in *Treasure Island,* lived for three years on goats, berries and oysters, and dreamed at nights of cheese, "toasted mostly," and woke up again to more oysters. This recipe is by a retired naval officer who would like to be marooned with lots of oysters.

MENU: *Willie's curried oysters*
Rice
EMBELLISHMENTS:
Chutney
Chopped raw onions
Sieved hard-cooked egg yolks
Crumbled cooked bacon
Watercress salad
Sherbet

WILLIE'S CURRIED OYSTERS:
4 tablespoons (½ stick) butter
2 medium onions, chopped
3 tablespoons flour
1½ cups half-and-half or plain milk
1½ tablespoons curry powder, preferably Madras brand
Salt, pepper

Sauté onions in butter until pale yellow but not browned. Sprinkle with flour and stir until blended. Add milk slowly, stirring until smooth and thickened. Add curry powder and seasonings. Cook the oysters separately in their juice just until the edges curl. Add oysters and juice to the onion sauce. Serves 4.

OYSTERS, HAM AND MUSHROOMS IN A CHAFING DISH

Chafing dishes are "in" again and do fit in with our present informal ways of serving. Because I do not myself like show-off cooking, I prefer recipes that can be prepared ahead and kept warm for serving in the chafing dish.

MENU: *Oysters, ham and mushrooms*
Noodles amandine
Hot biscuits
Orange and onion salad with watercress French
dressing

OYSTERS, HAM AND MUSHROOMS:
4 tablespoons (½ stick) butter
4 tablespoons flour
3 cups milk
1 cup cream
One light sprinkle of cayenne
Salt, pepper
1 quart oysters and liquor
2 cups diced cooked ham
1 pound mushrooms, sliced and sautéed in butter

Make a cream sauce by melting the butter, adding flour and cooking until almost dry. Add milk and cream, a little at a time, stirring constantly until smooth and thickened. Add seasonings. Simmer oysters in their own liquor until the edges curl. Add to the cream sauce with ham and sautéed mushrooms. Heat and let stand in the chafing dish. The longer this dish stands the better. That is within reason, of course. Serve with noodles amandine. Serves 6 to 8 generously.

OYSTER LOAF

This is popular in New Orleans and in San Francisco, where it is called a "peacemaker" or La Mediatrice. It is said to have been brought home in both places by husbands who have stayed out too late, as a peace offering to their wives. And, judging by the amounts sold, with plenty of beer, it has assuaged much feminine anger. Basically, it is a hollowed-out and toasted loaf of French bread filled with fried oysters or, sometimes in New Orleans, creamed ones. Both New Orleans and San Francisco claim to have originated this, but in an old English book of recipes published around 1600, there was mention of stewed oysters in rolls. Who's to say or who's to care? It is, indeed, delicious as a late snack with much cold beer and without ill feeling. My version is for creamed oysters because I do not like them fried. However, the recipe for fried oysters may be found on page 101.

MENU: *Oyster loaf*
        Beer
        Orange sherbet with Cointreau

OYSTER LOAF:
        1 fat 14-to-16-inch loaf of French or Italian bread, or 4
            Pepperidge Farm brown-and-serve loaves
        Butter

CREAMED OYSTERS WITH MUSHROOMS:
        1 pint oysters and juices
        ¼ pound mushrooms, sliced

4 tablespoons butter
3 tablespoons flour
1 cup of juice from the oysters and milk
½ cup light cream
1 teaspoon Worcestershire sauce
Salt

Slice top off bread. Pull out the soft insides, leaving a shell about a half-inch thick, and save the soft crumbs for another dish. Brush the inside of the bread with melted butter and also the inside of the top of the loaf. Toast in a 350° oven until lightly browned inside. Meanwhile, sauté drained oysters and mushrooms in 1 tablespoon of butter for 2 or 3 minutes. Set aside and keep warm. Melt the rest of the butter, add flour and cook until almost dry. Add oyster liquid and milk a little at a time, stirring constantly until smooth and thickened. Add cream a little at a time, stirring until blended. Season with Worcestershire sauce and salt to taste. (Some oysters are saltier than others.) Add oysters and mushrooms and turn into the toasted bread. Top with toasted lid. Serve hot. Serves 4.

OYSTERS BENEDICT

This is a variant of eggs Benedict, and I, for one, am not sure which I like the better. This dish is a little simpler to make when serving Sunday breakfast for a party, because the oysters can be simmered together, whereas it's difficult to poach a lot of eggs at the same time.

MENU: *Oysters Benedict*
Fresh asparagus
Pineapple sherbet with Bing cherries

OYSTERS BENEDICT:
>   4 thin slices of cooked ham or 8 slices of Canadian
>   bacon
>   1 pint oysters with their liquid
>   4 English muffins, halved and toasted
>   Hollandaise sauce

Sauté ham or Canadian bacon in a skillet. Remove and keep warm. Put oysters in a pan and cook just until the edges begin to curl and oysters are heated. Arrange two toasted muffin halves on each person's plate. Top each muffin half with a piece of ham or two pieces of canadian bacon overlapping. Put three or four oysters on each and cover with Hollandaise. Serve immediately. Serves 4.

HOLLANDAISE SAUCE: (quick version)
>   3 egg yolks
>   2 tablespoons lemon juice
>   ¼ teaspoon salt
>   Dash of cayenne
>   ½ cup butter (1 stick), heated to bubbling

Put egg yolks, lemon juice, salt and cayenne into an electric blender. Turn the motor on at low speed, and pour hot butter in gradually. Blend about 15 seconds, or until sauce is thick and smooth. Makes about ¾ cup.

OYSTERS ROCKEFELLER

No one can stand secrets. Antoine's in New Orleans has impressed three generations of devoted patrons with their Oysters Rockefeller by cannily refusing to give anyone the recipe. Many have tried to approximate the dish and most results are good if not identical to the original. This one is different in that it doesn't use spinach, but it aroused an appreciative gleam in Roy Alciatore's eye when he heard it. It uses Herbsaint, a New Orleans cordial that resembles the legally forbidden absinthe. Pernod which is available in more places has somewhat the same flavoring.

MENU: *Oysters Rockefeller*
Veal Milanese
Risotto with mushrooms
Roasted green pepper salad
Sesame seed bread
Wine sherbet

OYSTERS ROCKEFELLER:
    5 tablespoons unsalted butter
    2 tablespoons finely chopped parsley
    5 tablespoons finely chopped shallots
    1½ tablespoons finely chopped onion
    1 tablespoon finely chopped celery
    3 tablespoons fine stale bread crumbs
    Pinch of salt
    Few grains of pepper
    3 or 4 drops Tabasco
    3 or 4 drops Herbsaint
    24 fat oysters on the half shell (Southern ones are best
        for this, either from New Orleans or the middle Atlantic Coast, say the Rappahannock.)

Heat butter and add all other ingredients except the oysters. Cook over low heat until onions and celery are pale yellow. Remove from the heat, stir well. Heat 4 pie plates half-filled with rock salt. Arrange the opened oysters on their half shells, 6 to a tin. Spoon some of the mixture over each, dividing it as evenly as possible. Bake in an oven preheated to 425° until well-heated and the oysters plumped a bit. Serve each 6 oysters on their bed of hot salt. Serves 4.

OYSTERS KIRKPATRICK

After reading so many, many recipes that people think are Oysters Rockefeller, and that Roy Alciatore smiles at politely and says "Well, not exactly," it is a relief to have a recipe for Oysters Kirkpatrick from the Palace Hotel in San Francisco. This is the way they say the dish should be made. It is simple and unfussy to prepare and wondrously good.

MENU: *Oysters Kirkpatrick*
Sautéed zucchini
Baked potato with sour cream and chives
French bread
Crème Danica with more of the bread

OYSTERS KIRKPATRICK:
2 dozen oysters on the half shell
12 bacon strips, cut in half and partially cooked
1 cup catsup

Half fill 4 pie tins or other baking dishes with rock salt. Heat the salt in an oven preheated to 450° For each serving, arrange 6 oysters in their half shells on the hot salt. Spread a spoonful of catsup over each oyster and top with a strip of partially cooked bacon. Bake in hot oven 3-5 minutes. Serves 4.

OYSTERS BECHAMEL WITH TRUFFLES

It sounds rather irresponsible to blithely say "sprinkle with finely chopped truffles" when they are scarce and very, very expensive. The black ones are, but Italian white ones may be bought comparatively inexpensively and are good in a different way.

MENU: *Oysters Béchamel with truffles*
Peas with onions
Tiny new potatoes, cooked in their skins
Cherry tomatoes
Pear sherbet with shaved bitter chocolate

OYSTERS BÉCHAMEL WITH TRUFFLES:
1 pint oysters
BÉCHAMEL SAUCE:
3 tablespoons butter
3 tablespoons flour
1 cup chicken broth
Salt
Pinch of cayenne
Pinch of nutmeg
2 white truffles, cut in fine strips

Simmer oysters in their own liquid until edges begin to ruffle. Drain and cut in pieces. Make a sauce by melting the butter and adding flour. Cook until somewhat dry. Add the broth, a little at a time, stirring constantly until smooth and thickened. Add seasonings and blend well. Add oyster pieces and put in a small shallow casserole or individual baking shells. This amount will fill about 4 large shells or 6 medium size. Sprinkle tops with finely cut strips of truffle. Bake in a 325° oven just until hot, about 15 minutes. Serves 4–6.

BAKED OYSTERS, BOSTON STYLE

The Boston version is much like the Maryland, except that this has cheese, which is a nice touch.

MENU: *Baked oysters, Boston style*
Puréed peas
Rice pilaff with mushrooms
Cherry tomatoes
French bread
Watermelon sherbet

BAKED OYSTERS, BOSTON STYLE:
2 dozen raw oysters
4 slices whole wheat toast
4 slices ham
¼ cup butter, softened to room temperature
3 tablespoons freshly grated Parmesan, or Swiss cheese
1 tablespoon finely chopped parsley

Simmer oysters in their own juices until edges curl. Drain. Arrange slices of toast in a shallow casserole that fits them as neatly as possible. Place a slice of ham on each piece of toast and top with oysters. They will spread beyond each slice of toast, but that is all right. Cream butter and add cheese and parsley. Put a lump on top of each open sandwich, as it were. Put in a 400° oven just until cheese and butter mixture melts and runs and browns slightly. Serves 4.

OYSTERS WITH A FLORENTINE FINISH

This dish may be made with the frozen oysters.

MENU: *Oysters with a Florentine finish*
Corn fritters
Pickled celeriac
Fresh raspberries with pineapple chunks

OYSTERS WITH A FLORENTINE FINISH:
   2 dozen fresh or frozen oysters
   2 packages frozen creamed spinach (cooked according
      to package directions)

CHEESE SAUCE:
   2 tablespoons butter
   2 tablespoons flour
   1 cup chicken broth
   Salt, freshly ground black pepper
   1 egg yolk
   2 teaspoons grated Swiss and Parmesan cheese
   1 tablespoon butter
   More grated cheese

Simmer oysters in their own juice until edges curl. Cook spinach according to package directions. Make a sauce by melting butter and mixing with flour. Cook until somewhat dried. Add chicken broth, cooking and stirring constantly until smooth and thickened. Add seasoning and remove from the fire. Stir in the egg yolk, add cheese and blend well. Arrange spinach in a shallow buttered casserole. Strew oysters over it. Pour sauce over the oysters and spinach. Dot top of the casserole with butter and cheese. Bake in an oven preheated to 325° for 15 to 20 minutes. Serves 4–6.

STUFFED OYSTERS MORNAY

A voluptuous gilding of the lily.

MENU: *Stuffed oysters Mornay*
      Fresh asparagus
      Soufflé potatoes
      Fresh fruit in wine

STUFFED OYSTERS MORNAY:
> 2 dozen fresh, raw oysters, poached in their own juice
> 1 rock lobster tail
> ¼ pound fresh mushrooms, finely chopped
> 1 tablespoon finely chopped parsley

MORNAY SAUCE:
> 3 tablespoons butter
> 3 tablespoons flour
> 1 cup chicken broth
> Salt
> Pinch of cayenne
> Freshly grated Parmesan cheese

Remove oysters from their shells, carefully saving the juice. Put in a saucepan with juice and simmer until edges curl. Remove and drain. Meanwhile wash and dry the shells. Simmer rock lobster tail according to package directions, remove from shell and dice. Make a sauce by melting butter and cooking with the blended flour until somewhat dry. Add chicken broth, a little at a time, stirring constantly until thick and smooth. Add salt cautiously, tasting. (Some chicken broth has more than others.) Add cayenne. Mix sauce with the diced lobster, chopped mushrooms and parsley. Arrange an oyster on each shell in a casserole and spoon lobster-and-mushroom sauce over, rounding it neatly. Sprinkle with grated Parmesan. Bake in a medium oven, 325° for 10 to 15 minutes or until lightly browned. Serves 6–8.

OYSTERS CASINO

While I think that clams casino was the original dish, either bivalve is excellent baked this way.

MENU: *Oysters casino*
Baked potato
Mixed green salad with diced tomato, green onion,
cucumber, radish and French dressing
Lemon sherbet with mixed frozen fruit

OYSTERS CASINO:
2 dozen freshly opened oysters
2 slices bacon
⅓ cup finely chopped green onion
2 tablespoons finely chopped green pepper
2 tablespoons finely chopped celery
1 teaspoon lemon juice
1 teaspoon Worcestershire sauce
1 drop Tabasco sauce
4 pie tins half filled with rock salt

Arrange 6 oysters on the half shell on each pie tin half filled with rock salt. Sauté bacon until crisp and drain on paper towels. Sauté onion, green pepper and celery in the bacon fat. Cook until limp but not brown. Sprinkle with lemon juice, Worcestershire sauce and Tabasco. Spread this mixture on oysters in their shells, and crumble cooked bacon on top. Bake 10 minutes in an oven preheated to 400°. Serves 4.

OYSTERS ON A BED OF ONIONS

Rich and savory.

MENU: *Oysters on a bed of onions*
Puréed peas
Beet and endive salad
French bread
Sour cherry pie

OYSTERS ON A BED OF ONIONS:
>2 or 3 pounds of small white onions, sliced
>½ pint oyster juice
>Salt and pepper
>1 tablespoon butter
>About 40 blue point oysters
>Toast

There should be enough small onions to cover the bottom of the skillet. Pour oyster juice on the onions and simmer until they become transparent. Sprinkle with salt and pepper and dot with butter. Spread a thick covering of oysters over the melted butter and onion base. Cook uncovered for 5 minutes; cover, and cook until the edges of the oysters begin to ruffle. Cut in wedges and serve on toast. (A cake knife makes serving easy.) Serves 6.

THOMAS JEFFERSON'S PYE OF SWEETBREADS AND OYSTERS

Everything that Thomas Jefferson had interest in and touched took on style and grace, whether it was architecture, gardening, or food in its many wonderful guises. He was a Universal Man. This recipe has been called the most delicate pie ever made. The crust is made of puff paste which admittedly needs skill to make. Greek filo dough or strudel dough, both puff pastes, may be bought in frozen strips for use by the timid and inexperienced. Arrange strips in a rectangular baking dish, each overlapping the next a bit.

MENU: *Thomas Jefferson's pye of sweetbreads and oysters*
>*Fresh asparagus with butter*
>*Field salad or lambs lettuce with French dressing*
>*Hot biscuits*
>*Devil's food cake*

THOMAS JEFFERSON'S PYE OF SWEETBREADS AND OYSTERS:
  1 pie shell of puff paste, or filo or strudel dough
    (bought) or Pepperidge Farm frozen patty
    shells (bought)
  1 pair sweetbreads
  2 tablespoons lemon juice or vinegar
  1 pint oysters
  2 tablespoons butter
  2 tablespoons flour
  1 cup half-and-half
  3 egg yolks, well beaten
  Salt, pepper

Parboil sweetbreads in water with a couple of tablespoons of lemon juice or vinegar. Remove, plunge into ice water, drain and dice. Stew oysters in their own juices until the edges begin to curl. Remove from heat. In another saucepan, heat butter, add flour, and stir together until somewhat dried out. Add milk or half-and-half slowly, stirring constantly, until smooth and thickened. Remove from heat, add the three beaten egg yolks, salt and pepper, the cooked, diced sweetbreads, and stewed oysters with their juice. Turn into the puff paste shell, or line a shallow baking dish with the filo or strudel dough or patty shells. Top with crust, or dough, and bake until a delicate brown. Serves 4.

SCALLOPED OYSTERS

Since our great-grandmothers' time, or, for all I know, before that, scalloped oysters have been a festive and ceremonious staple, as well as a standby at church suppers. They are indeed simple to prepare, need brief cooking and are a simple thing to make well, provided the oysters are good.

MENU: *Scalloped oysters*
       Country ham
       Fordhook limas
       Hot biscuits
       Raspberry pie

SCALLOPED OYSTERS:

    1 quart oysters and their liquor
    1 1/2 cups bread crumbs or 2 cups cracker crumbs
    1/2 cup melted butter
    1/2 cup light cream
    Salt, pepper
    1 tablespoon Worcestershire sauce

Cover the bottom of a shallow buttered baking dish with a
layer of oysters, then some crumbs, oyster liquor, melted butter, salt and pepper. Repeat until all ingredients are used. Mix
the cream with Worcestershire sauce and pour over oysters.
Some like to add 2-3 tablespoons of sherry to the mixture. It
is nice but not obligatory. Bake in a 350° oven until thoroughly heated and the edges of the oysters ruffled, usually about
25-35 minutes, depending on the size and depth of the baking
dish. The fewer layers, the shorter time. The more layers, the
longer time and juicier dish. Serves 4-6.

SMOKED OYSTER OR SMOKED MUSSEL PUDDING

A sophisticated variant of the lox pudding served on the
Swedish Steamship Line and of the version made with anchovies, sometimes called silt pudding and other times Jans-
sen's temptation. It is a temptation in any of its versions.

MENU: *Smoked oyster or mussel pudding*
Tomatoes stuffed with chopped cucumber and
crumbled cooked bacon
Hot poppy seed rolls
Pear sherbet topped with shaved bitter chocolate

SMOKED OYSTER OR MUSSEL PUDDING:
4 medium-sized boiled potatoes, sliced
1 flat tin smoked mussels or oysters
2 cups light cream
2 eggs
2 sprigs fresh dill, chopped, or 1 teaspoon dill seed
No salt

Arrange a layer of potatoes in a shallow baking dish. Scatter a few smoked oysters or mussels over the potatoes, and repeat in layers ending with a layer of potatoes on top. Beat the eggs, add cream and beat some more or else put in an electric blender briefly. Add dill. Pour over potato mixture. Bake in an oven preheated to 325° for 45 to 50 minutes or until the dish looks custardy. Serves 4.

OYSTER, BACON AND CHIVE SOUFFLE

Any kind of shellfish can be souffléed this way. It is best to sauté oysters or diced meat—shrimp, crab, or lobster—in some butter with a little sherry before adding it to soufflé mixture.

MENU: *Gaspacho*
Oyster, bacon and chive soufflé
Succotash
Dried apricot soaked overnight in white wine and
served in it with a dollop of sour cream

OYSTER, BACON AND CHIVE SOUFFLÉ:

    3 tablespoons butter
    3 tablespoons flour
    1 cup wine and oyster liquor, mixed
    1/8 teaspoon nutmeg
    4 eggs, separated
    1/2 pint oysters, fresh or frozen, chopped
    2 tablespoons finely chopped chives
    2 slices bacon, well-cooked and crumbled

Melt butter, blend in flour and stir over low heat until almost dry. Add wine and oyster liquor, a little at a time, stirring constantly until smooth and thickened. Remove from fire. Add nutmeg, salt if needed, and egg yolks. Stir until well blended. Add oysters and chives. Beat egg whites until stiff and fold in gently. Turn into a buttered soufflé dish with straight sides. Sprinkle the top with crumbled bacon. Bake in a 350° oven until the top springs back when lightly touched, and is lightly browned, about 30 to 35 minutes. Serve immediately. Serves 4.

OYSTERS SKEWERED WITH BACON AND COOKED GIBLETS

Some of the most interesting combinations of food came about quite naturally because they were plentiful in some region. This dish is an excellent example. Both oysters and chickens abound in the Chesapeake Bay area. There are good country hams and bacon there, too.

MENU: *Oysters skewered with bacon and cooked giblets*
           Baked celery cooked in cream with parsley
           Brown rice
           Sliced tomatoes
           Hot biscuits
           Rhubarb pie

OYSTERS SKEWERED WITH BACON AND COOKED GIBLETS:
>   1 quart oysters
>   4-6 slices bacon cut in inch pieces
>   ½ pound hearts and gizzards
>   ½ pound chicken livers cut in serving pieces
>   Lemon juice
>   Butter
>   Toast

Trim fat from hearts and gizzards and simmer until tender in water to cover. Drain. Cut the gizzards in bite-size pieces. Sauté chicken livers in butter until barely brown. Cut into pieces. Thread on bamboo skewers, an oyster, a piece of bacon, a piece of gizzard, a piece of bacon, an oyster, piece of bacon, a chicken liver, a piece of bacon, and a piece of heart. Repeat on separate skewers until all the ingredients are used. Arrange on a rack in a shallow pan to catch the drippings and put under the broiler turning several times until brown, 5-7 minutes in all. Serve on toast with a sauce of the pan and oyster juices, butter and lemon juice. Serves 4.

OLYMPIA PEPPER PAN ROAST

Olympia oysters are tiny West Coast oysters which average thumbnail size for the oyster itself, with the shell about the size of a twenty-five-cent piece. They are ambrosial, and fabulously expensive even near their home waters. Eastern oysters are a little large for this dish, but can be used. Canned Japanese baby clams have a similar texture and size and may be used interchangeably.

MENU: *Olympia pepper pan roast*
> *Puffy spoonbread*
> *Garden lettuce with lemon cream dressing*
> *Hot poppy seed rolls*
> *Pear sherbet with shaved bitter chocolate*

OLYMPIA PEPPER PAN ROAST:

> 1 pint Olympia oysters or 1 can baby whole clams (10 ounce)
> ½ stick butter
> ¼ cup finely chopped onions
> ¼ cup finely chopped green pepper
> 2 tablespoons lemon juice
> 2 tablespoons catsup
> 1 teaspoon Worcestershire sauce
> Salt, pepper
> Toast

Heat oysters in their juice and cook until plump and drain. In another pan cook onion and green pepper in butter for 2 or 3 minutes. Add lemon juice, catsup, seasonings to taste and Worcestershire sauce. Stir, then add the oysters. Simmer a minute or two, remove from heat and serve on toast. Some prefer to do this last cooking in individual casseroles in the oven. Serves 4.

NOODLES OLYMPIA

Olympia oysters are incredibly small and delicate of flavor. Equivalent in size and delicacy are the baby whole clams from Japan that can be bought canned. Eastern oysters may be used for this recipe if cut in quarters.

MENU: *Noodles Olympia*
Tomato aspic
French bread
Wine jelly with macaroons

NOODLES OLYMPIA:
>1 package noodles, cooked
>Chicken broth
>⅓ cup butter
>⅓ cup flour
>3 cups liquid, milk and the juice from oysters or clams
>1 cup grated Swiss cheese
>Pinch of nutmeg
>Salt, white pepper
>1 pint Olympia oysters or Eastern oysters, quartered, or 2 ten-ounce cans baby whole clams
>Soft bread crumbs
>More butter

Cook noodles in chicken broth and drain. Melt the butter and add flour; cook until slightly dry. Add the liquid, a little at a time, stirring constantly until sauce is smooth and thickened. Put cooked, drained noodles in a shallow casserole. Pour the sauce over all and then arrange raw oysters or clams on top. Sprinkle with soft bread crumbs and strew cheese on top. Dot with butter and bake in a 350° oven until bubbling. The crumbs protect the oysters. Serves 4.

FRIED OYSTERS

This is, perhaps, the only way I don't like oysters, but presumably I am in a minority group. It seems to me much too drastic treatment for these delicate and lovely bivalves. They should, I think in my prejudiced way, have only brief cooking over very low heat, or, best of all, none.

MENU: *Fried oysters*
French fried potatoes
Cole slaw
Sliced tomatoes
Rum buns

FRIED OYSTERS:
2 dozen oysters
Salt, pepper, cayenne
2 eggs, slightly beaten
Cracker crumbs
Salad oil

Drain oysters and pat dry. Sprinkle with salt, pepper and cayenne on all sides. Dip in cracker crumbs, then in beaten egg, again in cracker crumbs. If time permits, let stand in the refrigerator for an hour. (If they are cold, the batter stays on better during frying.) Heat salad oil to 365° or hot enough to make a drop of water dance when flicked in. Fill frying basket, about 6 at a time, fry until golden brown, remove and drain on paper towels. Serve hot. Serves 4.

FRIED OYSTERS PARMESAN

I seldom cook or eat fried oysters, but when I do, I like them prepared this way, as they used to do them in the heyday of Delmonico's when it was at 14th and Fifth Avenue long, long ago. This is an adaptation from a fascinating tome published around the turn of the century.

MENU: *Fried oysters parmesan*
Zucchini baked with tomatoes, onion and celery
Onion rolls
Sour cream mousse with wine

FRIED OYSTERS PARMESAN:
>1 quart medium-sized raw oysters
>Freshly grated Parmesan cheese
>2 eggs, beaten with 2 tablespoons of cream
>Cracker crumbs
>Salt, pepper
>Oil for deep frying
>Lemon quarters

Pat oysters dry. Roll in Parmesan cheese until thoroughly coated. Dip in egg beaten with cream and then in bread crumbs. Place on a plate and chill in the refrigerator for about an hour. (The batter will stay on better.) Heat fat to 380°. Fry a few, about 6, at a time, until golden brown. Drain on paper towels and keep warm. Serve with more salt and pepper and lemon wedges. Serves 4 to 6, depending upon the size of the oysters and the eagerness of the eaters.

HANGTOWN FRY

There are many fascinating and conflicting explanations of how this West Coast dish got its name and how is an Easterner to say which is the right one? It is one of the most agreeable ways of eating fried oysters.

MENU: *Hangtown fry*
>*Broiled tomato halves*
>*French bread*
>*Brown Betty*

HANGTOWN FRY:
>6-12 oysters, drained
>Cracker crumbs
>1 egg, beaten

Butter
6 eggs
¼ cup milk
Salt, pepper
4 strips bacon, cut in thirds

Season oysters with salt and pepper. Dip in crumbs, then in beaten egg, then again in crumbs. Sauté oysters lightly in butter until golden brown. Beat six eggs with milk, salt and pepper. Pour over fried oysters in the skillet until the eggs are cooked and lightly browned. Fold over into a half circle if you can. If not, don't worry. Meanwhile, sauté the bacon and drain. Serve the omelet, for that is more or less what this is, and garnish with bacon curls. Serves 4.

OYSTERS BEIGNETS

Beignets are an elegant kind of fritter that starts out with a cream puff dough which is surprisingly simple to make. If you are nervous, although you shouldn't be, use prepared cream puff mix and go on from there.

MENU: *Oyster beignets with lemon and butter sauce*
Broccoli
Pineapple sherbet with fresh strawberries
Macaroons

OYSTER BEIGNETS:
2 dozen oysters
½ cup milk
½ cup strained oyster liquor
¼ cup butter
2 teaspoons salt
½ teaspoon sugar

1 cup flour
4 eggs
Fat for deep frying
3 tablespoons butter
3 tablespoons lemon juice

Simmer oysters in their own juices until the edges curl. Drain on towel. Chop fine. Bring to a boil the milk and oyster juice or all milk, ¾ cup butter, salt and sugar. Add flour all at once and cook, stirring all the while, until the mixture forms a smooth ball. There should be no flour or batter adhering to sides of pan. Remove from heat. Cool slightly before adding the eggs, one at a time and beating after each addition. Add drained, chopped oysters. Drop by spoonfuls into deep fat which has been heated to 375°. Fry until fritters are brown on all sides. They turn over in the fat as they cook. Drain on paper towels and serve hot with lemon and butter sauce, made by simmering 3 tablespoons of butter with lemon juice until they have become reduced. Serves 4.

OYSTER FRITTERS

Fritters come in and out of fashion, although they never get so far out that they don't find their way back. Electric deep-fat fryers and electric skillets with their controlled heat make fritters very easy to do these days. They are very tempting when properly crisp and crunchy.

MENU: *Country ham, sliced thin or Canadian bacon*
Oyster fritters
Baked sweet potatoes
Orange sherbet with macaroons

OYSTER FRITTERS:

2 dozen fresh or frozen oysters, cut in small pieces
1 cup milk
2 eggs, well beaten
1⅓ cups sifted flour
1½ teaspoons baking powder
Salt, pepper
2 tablespoons finely chopped parsley
1 tablespoon finely chopped chives
1 tablespoon finely chopped onion
⅓ cup butter (for frying)
⅓ cup butter, melted (for sauce)
3 tablespoons lemon juice

Mix milk with well-beaten eggs, flour, baking powder, salt, pepper, onion, parsley and chives and let stand at least two hours. (This can be mixed in an electric blender.) If so, add the parsley, chives and onion after removing from the motor.) Mix the oysters with this. Make into small cakes or drop from a spoon into hot butter in frying pan. Brown on both sides. Serve with a sauce made with melted butter and lemon juice. Serves 4–6.

OYSTER STUFFING FOR TURKEY

Sometimes the best part of a turkey roasted for a festive occasion was the stuffing. At least it seemed so when I was young and now often still does, many, many years later.

MENU: *Roast turkey with oyster stuffing*
Mashed potatoes
Creamed green peas and onions
Cranberries cooked in apricot liqueur
Lemon sherbet

OYSTER STUFFING: (For a 6-pound turkey; double the amounts
for a larger bird)
½ cup melted butter
1 teaspoon salt
1 teaspoon celery seed
1 teaspoon marjoram
Freshly ground black pepper
¼ cup chopped parsley
4 cups dry bread cubes or coarse crumbs
1 pint oysters drained and picked over to remove bits
of shell

Mix melted butter with salt, celery seed, marjoram, pepper
and parsley. Toss bread cubes or crumbs in this until fairly
well coated. Add a little oyster liquor if a moister dressing is
preferred. Add oysters and fill the bird with it, being careful
not to pack it too tightly. Roast according to standard directions.

QUAIL STUFFED WITH OYSTERS

This is one of the most elegant ways of presenting very, very
few oysters. Quail is one of the most delicate and delicious of
game birds and very simple to prepare.

MENU: *Quail stuffed with oysters on toast*
Fresh peas
Wild rice
Hot biscuits
Lemon curd tarts

QUAIL STUFFED WITH OYSTERS:
    4 quail
    4 large or 8 small oysters
    4 strips lean country-cured bacon
    4 slices of toast
    Paté

Put one or two oysters in each well-cleaned bird. Wrap each bird around the breast and body with one strip bacon. Roast in 350° oven for about 15-20 minutes or until no pink shows when pricked with a fork. Spread toast with paté and serve each quail on a piece of toast, juices and all. Serves 4.

AN OYSTER ROAST

With oysters in season from September until April this classic and traditional cookout, generally indigenous to the Eastern Coast, is most prevalent in cold weather when it is, of course, served indoors. When it is given by the local Fire Department or some other fund-raising group, this orgy is a rustic affair with newspapers—chosen for absorption and availability— used for covering tables, and with lots of paper napkins. There are professional shuckers for oysters eaten on the half shell, also a cook who prepares panned oysters, oyster stew, and fried oysters. Bowls of sauce made of chili sauce and freshly ground horseradish are placed at convenient intervals. Some like to dip oysters in this, but the true aficionado prefers to slurp them from the shells with no condiment needed. Oyster forks are available for the fastidious. Plenty of beer is there for everyone, with stalks of celery, salted crackers and large Pennsylvania pretzels on the side. The home version is a bit daintier, and the truly thoughtful host will see that there is a non-oyster dish for non-oyster eaters married to the dedicated ones.

MENU: *Raw oysters*
   Steamed and roasted oysters, melted butter
   Roasted corn
   Fried chicken, ham or steak
   Spoonbread
   Cole slaw with boiled dressing
   Key lime pie
   Beer (cold and plentiful)

Lots and lots of oysters are needed, the amount varying according to the presumed appetites and addiction. It will be many, many more than are eaten under normal circumstances. Dig a ditch, say about six feet, and build a fire the length of it. Over the fire lay a length of chicken wire. Cover this, more or less, with oysters in their well-scrubbed shells and ears of corn, from which the silk has been removed, in their dampened husks. Stuff a piece of butter in each husk and twist the husks tightly. Over this lay a piece of wet burlap and more oysters on top that will roast while those underneath steam away. Get your best oyster shucker to work (practice according to instructions given on page 75). Raw oysters are eaten while the others are roasting and steaming. The oysters are done when they open, but the corn will take 20 minutes or slightly longer. Each ear will need another lump of butter and, of course, salt. Serve with bowls of melted butter with a dash of Tabasco, for everyone to dip into. This traditional combination is possible in Maryland and Virginia with the first of the fall oysters and the last of the fresh corn in September.

Six · SCALLOPS

PERUVIAN SCALLOPS SEVICHE

Variants of this dish turn up in many places under many different names. You will find them in Mexico, Hawaii, and Japan, among other places. Basically, the citrus juices "cook" the sea food or at least the enzymes in the juice act in a chemical way upon it as heat does, and it becomes opaque. The boiling water that is poured on the scallops in a colander acts as a slight nudge.

MENU: *(cocktail accompaniements)*
Peruvian scallops seviche
Artichoke leaves with a dip of lightly seasoned yoghurt
Hot cheese puffs

PERUVIAN SCALLOPS SEVICHE:
2 pounds scallops, sliced paper-thin vertically
Juice of 7 lemons
Juice of 2 oranges
2 large onions, finely sliced

2 hot red peppers, cut in strips, or 2 dried hot red
    peppers, crumbled
Watercress
Small shells (miniature ones like those used for
    Coquilles Saint-Jacques)

Place sliced scallops in a large colander and pour about two
quarts of boiling water over them. Drain well. Place in a bowl
and cover completely with lemon and orange juice. (The
original recipe calls for sour oranges, which are not easily
available in most places, so these proportions are adjusted to
include more lemon juice.) Soak onions briefly in salted water.
Rinse and drain. Add onion and hot pepper to the bowl and
stir to distribute flavors. Cover tightly and keep in the refrigerator for at least four hours. To serve as a cocktail accom-
paniement, drain and place three or four slices of scallops on
a sprig of watercress in the miniature shells. Serve with oyster
forks or Japanese bamboo-handled ones.

COQUILLES SAINT JACQUES MAYONNAISE

A pleasing way to serve scallops cold.

MENU: *Coquilles Saint Jacques mayonnaise*
          Broiled chicken breasts
          Broiled tomato halves
          Cold whole artichokes with olive oil
          Watermelon half with fresh fruits

COQUILLE SAINT JACQUES MAYONNAISE:
    1 pound scallops, sliced
    1 cup court bouillon (p. 59)
    VINAIGRETTE SAUCE:
        ⅔ cups olive oil

> 3 tablespoons lemon juice
> 1 teaspoon paprika
> Salt, pepper
> 1 tablespoon finely chopped hard-boiled egg
> 1 teaspoon finely chopped green olives
> 1 tablespoon finely chopped capers
> 1 teaspoon finely chopped chives
> 1 teaspoon finely chopped parsley
> 1 teaspoon finely chopped pickle

Watercress
Mayonnaise
3 tablespoons capers

Simmer scallops in court bouillon for about 5 minutes or until opaque. Cool. Mix the ingredients for vinaigrette sauce. Drain scallops and chill in vinaigrette sauce for 20 minutes or until needed. Drain again and arrange on beds of watercress in scallop shells or on small salad plates. Coat with mayonnaise and sprinkle with the capers. Serves 4-6.

SCALLOPS WITH BUTTER AND VERMOUTH

One of the quickest and simplest and best of all ways of cooking scallops.

MENU: *Scallops with butter and vermouth*
      Creamed spinach
      Parsleyed new potatoes
      Orange and onion salad
      Coffee mousse

SCALLOPS WITH BUTTER AND VERMOUTH:
> ½ stick (⅛ pound) butter
> ¼ cup dry vermouth or dry white wine

1½ pounds scallops, preferably small bay scallops

Melt butter. Sauté scallops for 2 or 3 minutes, or until they are opaque—no longer. Add vermouth and keep over the heat just long enough to get it warm. Serve immediately. No other seasoning is needed. Serves 4.

SCALLOPS CHINESE STYLE

The Chinese way of seasoning and of cooking only briefly enhances many different foods, among them scallops.

MENU: *Scallops Chinese style*
Cold baked tomatoes stuffed with spinach
Rice
Hot herbed French bread
Cheesecake topped with blueberries

SCALLOPS CHINESE FASHION:
1½ tablespoons cooking oil
1½ pounds scallops, each cut in 4 round slices
2 teaspoons salt
1 green onion, cut in small pieces
2 slices fresh ginger
1 tablespoon cornstarch, mixed with 4 tablespoons
cold water

Heat the oil (not olive) in a skillet over high heat. Add scallops, stir for 1 minute, then add salt, scallion and ginger slices. Stir again for 2 minutes. Add cornstarch and water mixture. Stir for a minute or more until the juices in the pan become thickened and translucent and the scallops slices opaque. Serve immediately with rice. Dishes thickened with cornstarch should not be held long or done ahead. Serves 4.

SCALLOPS WITH BLACK BUTTER

Scallops are one of the shellfish wonders, needing no tedious preparation and only the briefest cooking. There is no waste, practically no calories, and some lovely nutritional assets. There are many, many ways of cooking them.

MENU: *Scallops with black butter*
Boiled new potatoes
Green beans with almonds
Boston lettuce salad
Pineapple milk sherbet

SCALLOPS WITH BLACK BUTTER:
½ cup wine vinegar or lemon juice
¼ pound unsalted butter
1 pound bay or sea scallops
⅓ cup parsley, finely chopped
2 tablespoons capers
Seasoned bread crumbs

Heat vinegar or lemon juice until reduced by half. Add butter and parsley. If sea scallops are used, cut into quarters. Add the scallops to butter and vinegar mixture and cook briefly, until opaque. Add capers, salt lightly and sprinkle with seasoned bread crumbs if desired. Serves 4.

COQUILLES SAINT JACQUES

One of the truly great seafood classics.

MENU: *Coquilles Saint Jacques*
Creamed spinach
Tiny new potatoes
Raspberry mousse

COQUILLES SAINT JACQUES:
> 1 pound scallops, fresh or frozen, quartered
> ½ cup dry white wine
> 1 small white onion, finely chopped
> ½ pound mushrooms, sliced
> 1 lemon
> 2 tablespoons butter
> 2 tablespoons flour
> ⅔ cup heavy cream
> Fine bread crumbs
> Grated Parmesan cheese

Cook scallops in white wine with the onion for about five minutes. Drain and save the liquid. Cook mushrooms in about half a cup of water with lemon juice. Drain and save the juice. Melt butter, add flour, and cook until almost dry. Blend in cream. Add wine from the scallops and juice from the mushrooms, stirring until smooth and thickened. Add scallops and mushrooms. Pile into scallop shells or ramekins. Sprinkle the tops with bread crumbs and Parmesan cheese. Put in a 400° oven until lightly browned. Serves 6.

SKEWERED SCALLOPS

Two pounds of scallops for four people is very lavish but less looks meager on the skewers.

MENU: *Skewered scallops*
Mixed rice and wild rice cooked in chicken broth with chopped green onions
Peas
Escarole salad
Mint parfait

SKEWERED SCALLOPS:
>   2 pounds scallops
>   Mushroom caps
>   Slices of bacon to match (4-5 strips cut in quarters)
>   ½ cup melted butter
>   Juice of 1 lemon
>   Salt, pepper
>   Bamboo skewers (soaked in water to keep from
>   burning)

Dip scallops and mushroom caps in melted butter and lemon juice. Thread scallops on skewers, alternating with bacon and whole mushroom caps, until the four skewers are loaded. Brush with remaining butter and lemon juice. Broil briefly, turning on each side until golden. Serve with rice and wild rice. Serves 4 generously.

FRIED SCALLOPS

Probably the best known and therefore presumably the favorite way of cooking and serving scallops.

MENU: *Fried scallops*
>   *French fried eggplant fingers*
>   *Cole slaw*
>   *Mixed melon balls with fresh blackberries*

FRIED SCALLOPS:
>   1 pound bay or sea scallops
>   2 eggs, slightly beaten
>   Bread crumbs
>   Salt, pepper
>   Fat for frying
>   Lemon wedges
>   Tartar sauce

Rinse scallops, drain and dry thoroughly. If sea scallops are used, cut in quarters. Beat the eggs with three tablespoons of cold water. Dip scallops in egg and then in bread crumbs to which salt and pepper have been added. Arrange breaded scallops on a plate and put in the refrigerator to chill for about an hour. (This makes the batter stay on better.) Fry until a light brown (3 to 4 minutes) in deep fat heated to 375°. Drain on paper towels, serve with tartar sauce and lemon. Serves 4.

BAKED SCALLOPS ON TOAST

This method of cooking scallops emphasizes their delicate and savory flesh.

MENU: *Baked scallops on toast*
Broccoli
Spoonbread
Watercress and grapefruit segments

BAKED SCALLOPS ON TOAST:
4 thick slices French bread, toasted
1 pound scallops, cut in quarters
½ cup white wine
3 tablespoons butter
3 tablespoons flour
1 cup milk
Juice from scallops and wine
Salt, pepper
Dry, coarse, fresh bread crumbs
Freshly grated Swiss cheese
Butter

Arrange toasted French bread in individual shallow baking

dishes. Simmer scallops in wine. Drain, reserving liquid, and placing on the toast. Make a cream sauce by melting butter, adding flour and stirring until well blended. Add, a little at a time, milk and the juice and wine in which scallops were cooked, stirring until smooth and thickened. Season with salt and pepper and pour over the scallops. Sprinkle the tops with bread crumbs and then grated cheese. Dot with butter. Bake in a 350° oven until brown and bubbling, about 20 minutes. Serves 4.

SCALLOP AND SPINACH QUICHE

A quiche, which is an "in" dish now, is a non-sweet custard pie with whatever you choose to put in it.

MENU: *Scallop and spinach quiche*
Cherry tomatoes
Hot biscuits
Fresh pineapple with sherbet

SCALLOP AND SPINACH QUICHE:
Pastry for a one-crust, 9-inch pie
1 pound spinach, cooked and chopped or 2 packages frozen chopped spinach, cooked
4 eggs
1 cup cream
Pinch of nutmeg
½ pound bay or sea scallops

Bake the pie shell five minutes in an oven preheated to 450°. Spread the spinach on bottom of pie shell. Beat eggs. Add cream and beat some more. Add seasoning and scallops. Reduce heat in the oven to 350°. Pour scallop mixture over spinach. Place in oven and cook until a knife inserted comes out clean, or about 15 to 25 minutes. Serves 4.

SCALLOPS A LA MARINIERE

A wonderfully simple way to serve scallops.

MENU: *Scallops à la marinière*
Broiled tomato halves
Hominy soufflé
Boston lettuce with Roquefort dressing with a bit of garlic
French bread
Strawberries Romanoff

SCALLOPS A LA MARINIERE:
1 pound scallops, cut in quarters
Salt
Freshly ground black pepper
3 tablespoons finely chopped mushrooms
1 tablespoon finely chopped parsley
1/4 cup white wine
2 tablespoons lemon juice
Fresh bread crumbs
Butter
Sprigs of parsley

Season scallops with salt and pepper. Toss lightly with chopped mushrooms and parsley. Fill four baking shells with this mixture. Mix white wine and lemon juice; divide among the four shells. Sprinkle tops with bread crumbs and dot with butter. Place in an oven preheated to 325° and bake about 10 to 15 minutes. Serve hot with a sprig or two of fresh, crisp parsley inserted at a dashing angle. Serves 4.

Seven · SHRIMP

BOILED SHRIMP

This is the basic recipe to use when a recipe calls for cooked shrimp and you prefer to cook them from scratch, rather than using frozen cooked or canned shrimp. Large packages of frozen raw shrimp, 2½ to 5 pounds, may be cooked ahead and kept in the freezer until needed.

MENU: *Boiled shrimp cocktail with sauce (catsup, Worcester-shire sauce, horseradish)*
Broiled lamb chops
Broccoli with Mornay sauce
Corn muffins
Sliced cucumbers and radishes in sour cream
Vanilla ice cream topped with frozen strawberries, slightly thawed

BOILED SHRIMP:
2 pounds raw shrimp
10 peppercorns

1 clove garlic, peeled and cut in half
1 lemon, sliced
½ teaspoon thyme
2 cloves
1 bay leaf
1 teaspoon celery seed or chopped leaves
2 teaspoons salt
Water to cover

Put shrimp and seasonings in a saucepan and add enough water to cover. Bring to a boil and simmer gently from 3 to 5 minutes, no more, just until shrimp turn pink. Remove from the water immediately and drain. Let cool. Peel off shells and remove the black vein down the back with the point of a knife. Rinse shrimp and chill until wanted. Serves 4–6.

SHRIMP FOR COCKTAILS

One recipe that is seldom needed is for what to do with left-over cocktail shrimp. Most people can eat any given amount. This recipe is given in proportions for one pound of shrimp. Adjust the quantities to your guests and your pocketbook. The flavors are a pleasing deviation from the usual. The shrimp may be drained on paper napkins before being arranged on a cake stand or a large compote covered with grape leaves or some other decorative greenery.

MENU: *Shrimp for Cocktails*
Roast beef
Yorkshire pudding
Bibb lettuce with lemon cream dressing
Lemon sherbet with chocolate leaves

SHRIMP FOR COCKTAILS:
   1 pound smallest size uncooked shrimp
   1 tablespoon mixed pickling spices
   2/3 cup olive oil
   1/3 cup dry French vermouth
   1 clove garlic, cut in 3 pieces
   Salt
   Freshly ground black pepper

Simmer shrimp in water with pickling spices until pink, about 3 to 5 minutes depending upon size. Drain, shell and devein if necessary. Mix oil, vermouth, garlic, salt and pepper. Pour over shrimp in a bowl and chill for several hours or overnight. Before serving, drain on paper towels and arrange on a dish (see above) that pleases the eye as well as being functional. Who knows how much cocktail shrimp serves how many?

SHRIMP CANAPES WITH DILL BUTTER

Shrimp gracefully disporting themselves on toast rounds are a little daintier to eat along with cocktails than the usual ones that are dipped, and canapés are scarcely more trouble to fix. Arrange ahead of time on small trays or lucite platters and cover with pliofilm wrap while chilling until needed.

MENU: *For cocktail accompaniments:*
        Shrimp canapés with dill butter
        Homemade almonds
        Tiny cream puffs filled with cream cheese and chive
        Cherry tomatoes
        Hot cheddar cheese puffs

SHRIMP CANAPÉS WITH DILL BUTTER:
Melba toast rounds
Dill butter
½ pound cooked shrimp, peeled and deveined

DILL BUTTER:
1 stick sweet butter, softened
1 tablespoon finely chopped fresh dill or 1 teaspoon ready-mix dill liquid
½ teaspoon lemon juice

Mix butter with dill and add lemon juice. If desired, mix in a drop or two, no more, of green coloring. Either spread the canapés with the butter or, with a little more dash and care, you can decorate the canapés with dill butter, using a pastry tube. Arrange several shrimp, depending on size, decoratively on each canapé.

TINY PUFF SHELLS WITH SHRIMP AND MUSHROOM PUREE

You may wish to make these tiny puff shells yourself or you can buy them 30 to a package. They should be about an inch in diameter and may be made either of puff paste or pie crust and should be baked before adding the filling. They make a delectable mouthful and are best warmed before serving.

MENU: *Tiny puff shells with shrimp and mushroom purée*
Veal piccata
Creamed spinach
Rice pilaf
Hot sesame rolls
Chocolate soufflé

TINY PUFF SHELLS WITH SHRIMP AND MUSHROOM PURÉE:
  MUSHROOM PURÉE:
        1 pound fresh mushrooms
        Salt, pepper
        ½ teaspoon grated lemon peel
        1 cup heavy cream
      Tiny puff shells
      Tiny cooked shrimp, peeled and deveined
      Finely chopped fresh dill (nice but not obligatory)

Put mushrooms in a blender, and flick the switch on and off two or three times until they are chopped; or chop with a knife until mushrooms are fine and saucelike. Drain and cook in a pan over low heat until their liquid evaporates. Add salt, pepper, lemon peel, and cream. Cook for 2 or 3 minutes. This makes about 1½ cups and may be kept in the refrigerator for a week or two and used in other dishes. To serve, fill each puff with a teaspoonful of mushroom purée and insert 1 or 2 shrimp, depending upon size. Warm in slow oven. Sprinkle with a bit of fresh dill if desired. Serve warm.

SPICED SHRIMP

This is one of those all-four-feet-in-the-trough dishes that is definitely not for the dainty. It is eaten leisurely, and blissfully, and messily, in raw bars in seafood restaurants and at home all around the Chesapeake. Shrimp are not caught in that region, but lots are eaten—mostly as an in-between snack and preferably with cold, cold beer. It is fine for those sudden and unscheduled hungers. Seafood restaurants in Washington, like the now defunct but much lamented New England Bar on the old waterfront, did not bother with finger bowls. There was a washbasin near the bar in the main room and when the customers finished with shrimp they just got up and washed their hands.

MENU: *Spiced shrimp and beer*

SPICED SHRIMP:
    1 cup vinegar
    1 cup beer
    1 crushed hot Italian or Spanish red pepper
    1 clove garlic, cut in half
    1 large onion, sliced
    1 teaspoon dry mustard
    1 teaspoon celery seed
    2 bay leaves
    6 cloves
    3 pounds raw shrimp, in their shells

Mix vinegar with beer and seasonings. Add two cups water
and simmer for one-half hour. Add shrimp a cupful at a time.
Simmer 5-8 minutes or until shrimp turn pink. Remove
shrimp from liquid and let both cool separately, otherwise
the shrimp will overcook. Return shrimp to liquid in a bowl
and chill overnight. To serve, remove from refrigerator, let
come to room temperature and drain. Serve in large bowls
about soup size. The shrimp are peeled as they are eaten.
Have extra bowls for the shells. A cocktail sauce is served in
a bowl suitable for dunking the shrimp in. To make the sauce,
mix 1 cup tomato catsup with 1 tablespoon Worcestershire
sauce (or to taste), 2 tablespoons prepared horseradish and a
dash of lemon juice.

SHRIMP ARNAUD

Count Arnaud's restaurant in New Orleans, now run by his
daughter Germaine Casenave Wells, is famous for this shrimp
dish, even among people who have never been to that city.
This is the recipe cut down to home size.

MENU: *Shrimp Arnaud*
Broiled chicken breasts, basted with butter and
  vermouth
Purée of fresh peas
Scalloped potatoes
Fresh rhubarb pie

SHRIMP ARNAUD:

¼ cup celery, chopped fine
¼ cup shallots, chopped fine (onion is not as delicate)
¼ cup finely chopped parsley
½ cup prepared mustard
½ cup vinegar
½ cup olive oil
½ cup crushed red pepper
1 tablespoon salt
2 pounds shrimp, cooked, peeled and deveined

Mix together all the ingredients except shrimp. Pour over the shrimp and marinate for several hours, under refrigeration. Serves 4 to 6 generously.

COLD SHRIMP SOUP

This is a seductively soothing soup on a hot, hot day.

MENU: *Cold shrimp soup*
Lamb chops
French fried zucchini
Sliced tomatoes sprinkled with fresh chopped dill
Large flat loaf of sesame seed bread
Honeydew melon with blueberries

COLD SHRIMP SOUP:

    1 pound shrimp, cooked, peeled and deveined
    2 cucumbers, peeled and diced
    1 medium-sized onion, cut in pieces
    2 teaspoons salt
    1 teaspoon dry mustard
    1/4 teaspoon black pepper
    1 teaspoon paprika
    1 quart cold buttermilk
    Fresh mint or dill for garnish

Put half the ingredients in blender at one time, blend until smooth; then blend remainder. Chill in the refrigerator until icy cold. Top with a sprig of fresh mint or dill. Serves 4.

SHRIMP COOKED IN SAFFRON BROTH

Saffron is indeed expensive, more so than any other seasoning, and why not? It takes an incredible amount of crocuses to make a pound of this. It does give food a warm and tempting color and a delicate and subtle flavor.

MENU: *Shrimp cooked in saffron broth*
       Rice cooked in chicken broth with grated onion,
         mushrooms and pimentos
       French bread
       Watermelon balls with fresh blackberries

SHRIMP COOKED IN SAFFRON BROTH:

    1 cup dry white wine
    1 whole small white onion
    1 stalk celery, chopped

½ teaspoon saffron threads
Juice of 1 lemon
1 tablespoon finely chopped parsley
1½ cups small shrimp in their shells, deveined

Simmer wine, onion, celery and saffron for about 10 minutes. Add shrimp and simmer for about 7 minutes longer. Remove shrimp from broth. Strain broth and put back shrimp. Serve shrimp in broth in individual bowls. Each person fishes the shrimp from the broth, peels it and eats, dipping it in broth. The shrimp could be peeled before cooking, but somehow they don't seem as tender as this way. Serves 4.

SHRIMP IN DILL AND BUTTER

Most of the time I prefer to shell shrimp before cooking. Shelled shrimp seems to absorb flavors better, the cooking time is briefer, and the fuss of shelling and the clutter are out of the way.

MENU: *Shrimp in dill and butter*
Yellow rice cooked in chicken broth with 2 tablespoons of butter
Bibb lettuce with lemon cream dressing
Hot biscuits
Brown Derby cake with grapefruit cream cheese icing

SHRIMP IN DILL AND BUTTER:

1½ pounds of shelled and deveined shrimp
4 tablespoons (½ stick) sweet butter
2 tablespoons of chopped fresh dill or 1 teaspoon of dill ready-mixed liquid seasoning

Heat butter and simmer shrimp with the dill not more than

2-5 minutes, or until they just turn pink. Serve immediately. Serves 4.

SHRIMP PILAU

This is a classic Southern shrimp dish and one of the best for day in and day out eating.

MENU: *Shrimp pilau*
Cucumber and watercress salad
Hot poppy seed rolls
Apricot fritters

SHRIMP PILAU:

4 strips bacon, cut in 1-inch pieces
1 cup rice
1 cup sliced onions
1 clove garlic, minced
1 can (No. 2) tomatoes
2 cups water
1 teaspoon salt
Dash pepper
1½ pounds fresh or frozen raw shrimp, shelled and deveined

Cook bacon over low heat in Dutch oven or large enameled pan until crisp. Remove, drain and reserve. To fat in pan, add rice, onions and garlic. Cook over low heat, stirring constantly, until rice is golden brown. Add tomatoes, two cups water, salt and pepper. Stir and blend. Add shrimp. Bring to boil. Cover and simmer 20 minutes, over low heat. Add bacon. Serve from pan, or transfer to a serving dish. Serves 4–6.

SHRIMP IN TOMATO AND MUSHROOM CREAM

A delicate and festive dish.

MENU: *Shrimp in tomato and mushroom cream*
Saffron rice cooked in chicken bouillon
Cucumber aspic
Hot poppy seed rolls
Raspberry shortcake

SHRIMP IN TOMATO AND MUSHROOM CREAM:
4 tablespoons (½ stick) butter
1 small onion chopped fine
¼ pound sliced mushrooms
1½ pounds raw shrimp, peeled and deveined
1 cup heavy cream
2 tablespoons Italian tomato paste
Salt, white pepper

Sauté onion in butter until pale yellow. Add mushrooms and then shrimp and cook 2 to 3 minutes. Stir in tomato paste and cream. Simmer for 5-10 minutes, being careful not to let it come to a boil, and stirring from time to time. Serve with saffron rice. Serves 4.

SHRIMP IN WINE AND SOUR CREAM SAUCE

Russians, who also get infected by the same mania for crayfish which seizes the Scandinavians each year, cook their crayfish, shells and all, in this sauce. Lacking crayfish, this sauce is fine when cooked, shelled shrimp are briefly warmed in it.

MENU: *Shrimp in wine and sour cream sauce*
Fresh peas
Wild rice
Portuguese bread
Fresh pineapple

SHRIMP IN WINE AND SOUR CREAM SAUCE:
¾ cup dry white wine
1½ cups sour cream
1 teaspoon thyme
½ teaspoon salt
1½ pounds jumbo shrimp, cooked, peeled and
deveined

Simmer wine, sour cream, thyme and salt for 15 minutes, being careful not to let it come to a boil. Add shrimp, still over low heat, and simmer for 10 minutes or until the shrimp are warm. Serve with wild rice. Serves 4.

SHRIMP IN ORANGE SAUCE

This dish is shrimp at its most delicate best.

MENU: *Shrimp in orange sauce*
Yellow rice
Creamed spinach
Hot biscuits
Old-fashioned Concord grape pie

SHRIMP IN ORANGE SAUCE:
1½ pounds uncooked shrimp, peeled and deveined
1 tablespoon grated orange rind

1 cup orange juice
½ cup grapefruit juice
2 teaspoons salt
1½ teaspoon dry mustard
¼ teaspoon black pepper
6 drops Tabasco
2 tablespoons butter
3 tablespoons flour

Marinate shrimp in fruit juices, grated rind and seasonings overnight in the refrigerator. Drain and save the marinade for a sauce. Broil shrimp or pan-fry in butter 3 to 5 minutes or until barely pink. Drain and keep warm. Cook butter with flour in a pan until dry. Add juices slowly, stirring constantly until smooth and thickened. Add more seasoning if desired. Put shrimp in the sauce, reheat if necessary and serve over yellow rice cooked in chicken broth. Serves 4.

SHRIMP FLAMBE

A wave of pyromania seems to be sweeping the cooks in this country. Some of the most unlikely dishes go up in very pretty flames. Correctly, flambéing is used to give an unsweet kind of caramelizing—to describe it in somewhat contradictory terms. Then, it is good; other times, rather silly.

MENU: *Shrimp flambé*
Buttered noodles
Spinach salad
Hot biscuits
Lemon soufflé

SHRIMP FLAMBÉ:
2 pounds raw shrimp, shelled and deveined

¼ cup sweet butter
½ cup garlic
1 teaspoon grated onion
¼ cup applejack or apple brandy
¾ cup cider
¾ cup heavy cream
Salt, white pepper

Sauté salt, white pepper, shrimp and garlic in butter for about 5 minutes. Remove from heat, discard garlic and pour the heated applejack over shrimp. Light and while flaming, baste shrimp with the liquid. When the flame dies down, pour cider over shrimp and simmer 3 minutes. Add cream and blend well. Season with salt and white pepper. If desired, thicken the sauce by mixing flour with water and cooking a minute or two. Serve over buttered noodles. Serves 4.

SHRIMP CREOLE

Almost anyone can make this and almost everyone likes it. It is filling but not fattening and does not take much time or preparation.

MENU: *Shrimp creole*
Rice
Fresh diced pineapple with fresh strawberries

SHRIMP CREOLE:
4 tablespoons bacon drippings
1 garlic clove, minced
1½ cups celery, chopped
1 green pepper, coarsely chopped
1 large can Italian plum tomatoes
3 tablespoons tomato paste

1 teaspoon sugar
3 cups cooked shrimp, peeled and deveined
Salt and pepper to taste

Sauté onions, green pepper, garlic and celery in bacon drippings, for 15-20 minutes. Add tomatoes, sugar and tomato paste. Simmer slowly for 30-45 minutes until the mixture is thick in consistency. Add salt and pepper. About 15 minutes before serving, add shrimp. Serve over steamed rice. Serves 4-6.

QUENELLES DE BROCHET

This is a simplified version of a classic French dish. Pike quenelles may be made easily these days in an electric blender; even more easily and quickly a can of Norwegian fish balls can be opened and used. These fish balls are delicate in texture and perhaps less caloric than the traditional quenelles.

MENU: *Quenelles de Brochet*
Creamed spinach
Buttered noodles with poppy seeds
Sliced tomatoes, sprinkled with chopped basil
Hot biscuits
Vanilla pudding made with 1 teaspoon orange peel
and topped with shaved bitter chocolate

QUENELLES DE BROCHET:

1 small can (14 ounce) Norwegian fish balls
1 can frozen condensed cream of shrimp soup
½ cup white wine
1 cup frozen, peeled and deveined shrimp, or 1 can (5 ounce) deveined and drained
½ teaspoon dried tarragon
Salt and pepper to taste

Heat the fish balls, shrimp soup, wine, shrimp and terragon together. Just before serving check your seasoning and add salt and pepper if desired. Serves 4.

SHRIMP MARENGO

The original dish, concocted for Napoleon after the battle of Marengo, was made with chicken, but shrimp and chicken are pleasantly interchangeable in many dishes.

MENU: *Shrimp Marengo*
Barley Pilaf
Artichokes, served cold with olive oil to dip leaves in
Large sesame seed wafers crisped in the oven
Baked raspberry turnovers (bought frozen)

SHRIMP MARENGO:
6 slices bacon, cut into pieces
1 clove garlic, minced
1 cup chopped onions
1 pound mushrooms, sliced
1 large can (2 pound, 3 ounce) Italian-style plum tomatoes
1 can (6 ounce) tomato paste
1 can (10½ ounce) chicken broth
1 teaspoon monosodium glutamate
1¼ teaspoons oregano
1¼ teaspoons crushed basil
1 bay leaf
1 tablespoon salt
1 tablespoon sugar
¼ teaspoon black pepper
3 or 4 drops Tabasco
2 pounds raw shrimp, chilled and deveined

Sauté bacon in a large, deep, enameled pan or Dutch oven until crisp (an iron pan will turn the tomatoes dark). Remove and drain on absorbent towels. Sauté garlic and onion in bacon drippings until tender and opaque but not browned. Add mushrooms and cook for about 5 minutes. Add tomatoes, tomato paste, monosodium glutamate, chicken broth, oregano, basil, bay leaf, salt and pepper, sugar and Tabasco. Bring to a boil and simmer uncovered for about 20-30 minutes. Add shrimp and cook about 5-10 minutes or until shrimp are barely done. The sauce may be done ahead of time and the shrimp cooked in the reheated sauce at the last moment. Serves 4-6.

SHRIMP CANTONESE

There is, of course, lobster Cantonese. It is even better known, and more costly, too, than this shrimp version. This is the way Sou Chan who is head of the deservedly popular House of Chan Restaurant at 52nd Street and Seventh Avenue in New York taught me to make it.

MENU: *Shrimp Cantonese*
Rice
*Pickled or marinated celeriac or celery root (this may
be bought canned)*
Sour cream wine mousse

SHRIMP CANTONESE:
   2 pounds raw shrimp
   2 tablespoons oil
   ½ clove garlic
   Salt
   ½ pound fresh pork, chopped fine
   2 tablespoons soy sauce

½ cup hot water
1½ tablespoons cornstarch mixed with cold water
2 eggs

Shell the shrimp and split them down the back but not all the way through. Wash well and drain. Put oil into hot frying pan. Add garlic and salt. Brown. Remove the garlic and add chopped pork. Stir well over low heat until brown. Add soy sauce. Stir some more and add shrimp. Stir again and add hot water, cover and boil for 3 minutes. Add the cornstarch mixture slowly. Stir. Crack and drop the eggs over all. Stir slowly for ½ minute before serving. Serves 4.

SHRIMP CURRY

Shrimp adapts as gracefully to a curry sauce and all the embellishments as does lamb or chicken. Try to find a dish or several small matching dishes that will present these extras dramatically. One I have liked is a fan-shaped tortoise-shell dish with five or six indentations.

MENU: *Shrimp curry with rice*
      EMBELLISHMENTS:
        ½ cup chopped parsley
        2 cucumbers, peeled, diced with sweet and sour
          sauce
        Moist grated cocoanut
        Diced, peeled, ripe tomatoes
        Crumbled cooked bacon
        Chutney
        Chopped peanuts
      Tossed green salad with French dressing
      French bread
      Whole peaches in champagne

SHRIMP CURRY:

4 tablespoons (½ stick) butter
½ clove garlic, minced
1 medium onion, chopped
1 large apple, coarsely chopped
¼ cup shredded coconut
1½ tablespoons curry powder, preferably Madras
    brand, or use curry to taste
1½ tablespoons flour
1 inch piece fresh ginger, chopped, or ½ teaspoon
    powdered ginger
½ teaspoon dry mustard
2 cups chicken broth
1 cup cream
2 pounds raw shrimp, peeled and deveined, or
    Chilean languistinos

Sauté garlic, onion and apple in butter. Sprinkle with coconut, curry powder and flour. Stir until mixed. Add ginger and mustard and blend. Stir in chicken broth a little at a time and cook over low heat for an hour if possible. Add shrimp and cream and cook about 5 minutes. This may be done ahead of time and reheated with the cream before serving. Serve with rice and all the trimmings. Serves 4.

SHRIMP VIENNESE

This is the version of Geza Kiss who used to be chef at Hapsburg House in New York before he went on to the Hotel Weylin. Both places have served this.

MENU: *Shrimp Viennese*
Rice cooked in chicken broth
Belgian endive with oil, salt and pepper for dipping
Bobos torte

SHRIMP VIENNESE:

6 large mushroom caps, diced (or about ⅔ cup
  chopped mushroom stems)
1 tablespoon finely chopped onion
¼ pound (1 stick) sweet butter
1 tablespoon flour
1 tablespoon fresh chopped dill or 1 teaspoon dried
  dill
½ cup chicken consommé
½ cup cream, light or heavy
Juice of ½ lemon
Salt and pepper
1 tablespoon white wine
1½ pounds shrimp, cooked, peeled and cleaned

Sauté the mushroom and onion in a little of the butter. Add
flour, dill, consommé and cream. Bring to a boil. Add salt,
pepper, lemon juice and wine. Add shrimp and simmer over
low heat until the thickness of thin cream sauce. Add the rest
of the butter in small pieces and stir until melted, but do not
boil. Serve with rice. Serves 4-6.

NASI GORENG

This East Indian dish of Dutch origin is traditionally made
with very dry cooked rice, often cooked the day before and
dried so that each kernel is separate. This recipe makes it
more like a risotto, although using the traditional ingredients.
Nasi goreng is served topped with lengthwise strips of cucumber and often with a fried egg on each serving.

MENU: *Nasi Goreng*
       French bread
       Apple Soufflé

NASI GORENG:
> 1 stick butter
> 2 tablespoons Madras curry powder
> 1 medium onion, chopped
> 1 sweet green pepper, chopped
> 1 cup uncooked rice
> 2 cups chicken broth
> 1 pound cooked shrimp, peeled and deveined, or
>   2 cans (5 ounce) shrimp, minced and drained
> ½ cup diced ham or chicken
> 1 cup tiny meatballs (fresh and sautéed, or canned
>   Swedish meatballs with dill)

Melt butter and add curry powder. Cook for a minute or two to release the wonderful aroma. Add onion, green pepper and rice to this butter mixture. Cook for about 5 minutes, then add chicken broth, shrimp and ham or chicken. Bring to a boil, turn the heat down, cover and cook 20 to 25 minutes over low heat without removing the cover. Remove the lid, add meatballs and fluff with a fork. Let stand 5 minutes before turning into serving dish. Serves 4.

CURRIED SHRIMP WITH ZUCCHINI

Almost any shellfish tastes good with almost any kind of squash or with eggplant. Each delicate flavor complements the other. This dish with curry in it has the usual delicacy but a little more zip.

MENU: *Curried shrimp with zucchini*
Spoonbread
Pickled watermelon rind
Watercress and endive salad
Lemon sherbet with fresh strawberries

CURRIED SHRIMP WITH ZUCCHINI:

    4 medium zucchini, sliced but not peeled
    3 tablespoons bacon fat
    1 small onion, chopped
    1 tablespoon curry powder
    2 tablespoons flour
    Salt, pepper
    ½ cup undiluted evaporated milk
    2 cups cooked, cleaned shrimp

Cook zucchini in ½ cup water for about 10 minutes. Drain. Sauté onion in bacon fat. Add curry powder and stir awhile until wonderfully aromatic. Add flour, salt, pepper and milk, gradually, stirring constantly until smooth and thickened. Add shrimp. Arrange a layer of about half the zucchini in a shallow casserole. Pour in half the shrimp mixture, add the rest of the zucchini and top with the rest of shrimp mixture. Bake in a 350° oven until brown and bubbly. Serves 4.

SHRIMP FRIED RICE

The good old standby in most Oriental restaurants.

MENU: *Shrimp fried rice*
           Cucumber in yoghurt with chopped mint
           Sesame seed rolls
           Chocolate meringues with orange sherbet

SHRIMP FRIED RICE:

    2 tablespoons fat
    ½ clove garlic, minced
    1 bunch spring onions, tops and bottoms, chopped
    1 pound shrimp, cooked, peeled and deveined and cut

into 1-inch pieces, or 2 cans (5 ounce), rinsed and
drained
¼ cup tomato catsup
2 cups cooked rice
1 egg, lightly beaten
Salt and pepper

Sauté garlic, onions, and shrimp in melted fat. Cook for 2-3
minutes. Add catsup and mix well. Stir in cooked rice and
blend well. When rice is well heated, add the lightly beaten
egg and mix well. Remove from heat. The heat of the mixture
will cook the egg. Serve warm. Serves 4.

PIERRE'S SCAMPI

Pierre's scampi, like most of the dishes concocted by Hugo
Wrenn, the chef at Pierre's Restaurant on East 53rd Street in
New York, is consistently good.

MENU: *Pierre's scampi*
Baked eggplant with anchovies and bacon
Avocado and watercress salad
French bread
Individual strawberry tarts

PIERRE'S SCAMPI:
1½ pounds jumbo shrimp, split halfway down the
back but not peeled
White wine to cover
½ clove garlic, minced
1 bay leaf
2 or 3 thin strips lemon peel with the white bitter
part removed
1 dried hot red pepper, crumbled
12 whole peppercorns

¼ pound (1 stick) unsalted butter
Paprika
Juice from the marinade

The shrimp are marinated at least 24 hours in white wine, garlic, bay leaf, red pepper, peppercorns and a few strips of lemon peel without the white. To broil, remove from marinade, arrange on a baking sheet, dot with butter and paprika and broil from 12-14 minutes under the broiler, basting with a little of the juice from the marinade. Serves 4.

SHRIMP TERIYAKI

Strips of beef or chicken are also marinated and broiled this way, allowing more time for chicken. Perhaps beef teriyaki is best known to Americans. This is an untraditional version.

MENU: *Shrimp teriyaki*
Boiled new potatoes
Green peas
Romaine lettuce with French dressing
Fresh pineapple chunks

SHRIMP TERIYAKI:
2 pounds shrimp
2 cloves garlic, crushed
½ cup soy sauce
½ teaspoon dry mustard
2 tablespoons chili sauce
½ cup sherry
½ cup salad oil
1½ tablespoons sugar
2 teaspoons red wine vinegar
1 teaspoon grated fresh ginger or 1 tablespoon
preserved ginger, minced

Shell and devein shrimp, leaving tails intact. Rinse and dry with paper towels. Mix the remaining ingredients. Bring to a boil. Pour over shrimp and marinate 2 hours or longer. String shrimp on skewers. Broil over charcoal or in oven broiler until tender and glazed, basting frequently, with the marinade. It takes about 5 to 10 minutes, depending on size of shrimp and the amount of heat. Serves 4.

SHRIMP CASSEROLE

This is a dish that behaves itself well when cooked in large amounts and/or when cooked ahead. It may be cooked ahead and chilled for about 4 hours or overnight.

MENU: *Shrimp casserole*
Asparagus salad with hard-cooked eggs
Pepper rolls
Blueberry cheesecake

SHRIMP CASSEROLE:

2½ pounds raw shrimp, shelled and deveined
1 tablespoon lemon juice
3 tablespoons olive oil
1 cup rice
2 tablespoons butter
¼ cup chopped green peppers
¼ cup onion, chopped
1 teaspoon salt
⅛ teaspoon cayenne pepper
¼ teaspoon black pepper
⅛ teaspoon mace
1 can (10½ ounce) cream of tomato soup (condensed and undiluted)
1 cup heavy cream

¼ cup slivered, blanched almonds

Sprinkle shrimp with lemon juice and sauté in olive oil. Cook rice in 2 cups water. Bring to a boil. Cover and cook over low flame for 18 minutes. Sauté the green pepper and onion in butter. Add salt, pepper, mace and cayenne pepper. Then mix shrimp, rice, peppers and onions, seasonings, tomato soup and cream together in a 2-quart casserole. Top with almonds. Chill for at least 4 hours or overnight. Allow casserole to come to room temperature, then bake for an hour or more in an oven preheated to 350°. Serves 6-8.

LOUISIANA JAMBALAYA

A jambalaya is almost never made twice the same way. Basically it is a rich and aromatic rice and vegetable stew with ham, chicken, shrimp, crab meat, or what have you, and all versions are good.

MENU: *Louisiana jambalaya*
French rolls
Bowl of grapefruit segments, sliced hearts of palm,
    white grapes and curly endive with French dressing
French vanilla ice cream with hot fudge sauce

LOUISIANA JAMBALAYA:
3 slices bacon, diced
1 clove garlic, minced
1 medium onion, chopped
½ green pepper, chopped
1 tablespoon chopped parsley
1 cup uncooked rice
1 can (16-ounce size) tomatoes
Bay leaf

1 lump of concentrated chicken broth from a package
of Lipton's dehydrated chicken-noodle soup
1 pound fresh, uncooked shrimp, shelled and deveined,
or 2 cans (5 ounce size) shrimp, drained
1 dozen oysters, plus their liquid
¼ teaspoon Tabasco sauce
Salt to taste

Sauté bacon until some of the fat cooks out in the pan. Add
garlic, onion, green pepper and parsley to bacon fat and cook
until tender but not brown. Add rice, tomatoes in their liquid,
concentrated chicken broth, bay leaf, shrimp, oysters and their
liquid, and Tabasco sauce. Put into a large casserole, cover
and bake in a 350° oven until the rice is tender, about 1¼
hours. This may be partially cooked ahead of time. Serves 4.

SHRIMP AND MUSHROOM IN SHELLS

This dish is baked in the kind of shells used for Coquilles
Saint Jacques.

MENU: *Shrimp and mushroom in shells*
Noodles almandine
Cucumbers in sour cream with fresh dill
Butterflake rolls
Baked orange custard with macaroons

SHRIMP AND MUSHROOM IN SHELLS:

1 pound fresh or frozen, uncooked shrimp, peeled and
deveined
3 tablespoons butter
¼ pound fresh mushrooms, sliced through caps and
stems
2 tablespoons flour

1 teaspoon prepared mustard
¾ cup light cream or half-and-half
1 can (5 ounce) shrimp
2 tablespoons brandy
Salt to taste
Colonna's seasoned bread crumbs
More butter

Sauté mushrooms in 1 tablespoon butter. In another pan melt 2 tablespoons butter and blend flour and mustard with it. Add cream slowly; then add brandy, stirring until smooth and thickened. Add salt to taste, the sautéed mushrooms and the shrimp. Divide into 4 baking shells or individual casseroles or one shallow baking dish. Sprinkle top with bread crumbs and dot with butter. Bake in an oven preheated to 350° about 20 minutes or until top is brown and bubbling. Serves 4.

MRS. REARDY'S SHRIMP AND ARTICHOKE CASSEROLE

Possibly many jangled nerves have been soothed by this dish that is served at luncheons given by Adlai Stevenson to foreign colleagues at the United Nations.

MENU: *Mrs. Reardy's shrimp and artichoke casserole*
Rice
Tossed green salad
Fresh orange segments topped with melted orange marmalade and a blob of sour cream, and chilled

MRS. REARDY'S SHRIMP AND ARTICHOKE CASSEROLE:
¾ stick butter
¼ cup flour
¾ cup milk
¾ cup heavy cream

Salt and freshly ground black pepper to taste
1 No. 2 can artichoke hearts, drained, or 1 package
    frozen artichoke hearts (cooked according to direc-
    tions on package)
1 lb., shrimp, cooked, peeled, deveined
¼ cup fresh mushrooms, sliced
¼ cup dry sherry
1 tablespoon Worcestershire sauce
¼ cup freshly grated Parmesan cheese
Paprika

Melt a half-stick of butter and stir in flour. Cook a minute or
two, then add milk and cream a little at a time, stirring constantly with a wooden spoon or a whisk. When mixture is
smooth, add salt and pepper to taste. Arrange artichoke hearts
in a shallow, buttered baking dish. Scatter shrimp over the
artichoke hearts. Cook mushrooms in the remaining butter for
about 6 minutes. Spoon them over the shrimp and artichokes.
Add sherry and Worcestershire sauce to cream sauce and pour
over shrimp and artichokes. Sprinkle with Parmesan cheese
and paprika and bake about 40 minutes. Serves 4-6.

SHRIMP DE JONGHE

One of Chicago's best-loved dishes.

MENU: *Shrimp de Jonghe*
       Fried green tomatoes
       Spoonbread
       Romaine and watercress salad with vinaigrette
         dressing
       Chocolate mousse

SHRIMP DE JONGHE:

    ½ cup butter (1 stick), softened at room temperature
    1 teaspoon salt
    1 clove garlic, minced
    ⅔ cup fine, dry bread crumbs
    2 tablespoons finely chopped parsley
    ⅓ cup sherry
    ⅛ teaspoon cayenne pepper
    1 teaspoon sweet red Hungarian paprika
    2 pounds cooked shrimp, peeled and deveined

Mix softened butter with salt, garlic, bread crumbs, parsley, sherry and seasonings. Arrange shrimp in a shallow casserole and top with the crumb mixture, spreading so it covers all the shrimp. Bake in a 375° oven 20 to 25 minutes or until the topping has melted over the shrimp and becomes lightly browned. Serves 4 to 6.

SHRIMP FOO YUNG

Shrimp Foo Yung is more or less a Chinese shrimp omelet, although the proportions of shrimp to the eggs means using the word "omelet" rather loosely.

MENU: *Shrimp foo yung*
       Rice
       Strawberry and rhubarb pie

SHRIMP FOO YUNG:

    3 tablespoons fat
    1½ pounds raw shrimp, peeled and deveined
    1 tablespoon cornstarch
    2 tablespoons sherry

2 tablespoons soy sauce
2 or 3 slices fresh ginger (if obtainable)
1 small onion, chopped fine
¼ cup ground pork
2 eggs, beaten

Heat fat in a skillet until very hot. Add shrimp, cornstarch, sherry, soy sauce, ginger, onion and the pork. Stir and fry about 5 minutes. Then add the eggs and fry 3 minutes more, stirring all the while. Serve immediately. Serves 4.

SHRIMP SOUFFLE

A little like finding the pot of gold at the end of the rainbow.

MENU: *Shrimp soufflé with hearts of artichokes*
Fresh asparagus
Hot biscuits
Cheesecake with strawberry topping

SHRIMP SOUFFLÉ:
3 tablespoons butter
3 tablespoons flour
1 cup milk
2 tablespoons white wine
Salt, white pepper
1 teaspoon chopped fresh tarragon or ½ teaspoon dried
1 cup cooked shrimp, peeled, deveined and blended or ground
2 drops red vegetable coloring
1 drop yellow vegetable coloring
4 eggs, separated
1 package cooked, frozen artichoke hearts or 1 can, drained

Melt butter, add flour and cook until almost dry. Add the liquid a little at a time, stirring until smooth and thickened. Season with salt, pepper and tarragon. Stir in egg yolks and then the drops of coloring, if used. Use very, very cautiously. It should be a very pale delicate pink, not a lurid one. Stir in ground shrimp. Arrange artichoke hearts on the bottom of a buttered soufflé dish. Beat egg whites until stiff. Fold into shrimp mixture gently and pour on top of the artichoke hearts. Bake in an oven preheated to 350° for 30 to 40 minutes. Serves 4.

CHEESE SOUFFLE WITH LANGUISTINOS

A variation on Madame Prunier's cheese and crayfish served in her famous London seafood restaurant.

MENU: *Cheese soufflé with languistinos*
       Fresh peas and mushrooms
       Hot biscuits
       Vanilla ice cream with broiled freestone peaches

CHEESE SOUFFLÉ WITH LANGUISTINOS:
    3 tablespoons butter
    3 tablespoons flour
    1 cup milk
    ½ cup freshly grated Parmesan
    ½ cup freshly grated cheddar
    Salt
    ¼ teaspoon finely grated nutmeg
    3 eggs, separated
    ¼ pound mushrooms, sliced
    2 tablespoons butter
    1 package frozen Chilean languistinos, thawed

Melt butter, add flour and cook until almost dry. Add milk a little at a time, stirring until smooth and thickened. Add cheese and seasonings. Stir in the yolks of eggs. Blend until smooth. Whip the egg whites until stiff and fold into the cheese mixture gently. Sauté mushrooms in butter until lightly brown. Put a layer of mushrooms and languistinos in a buttered soufflé dish. Pour in some of the soufflé mixture, then more of the languistinos and mushrooms. Top with the rest of the soufflé. Bake in an oven preheated to 350° for 40-45 minutes or until the soufflé springs back when lightly touched. Serve immediately. Serves 4.

SHRIMP AND CHEESE PIE

Shrimp in one of its sturdier guises.

MENU: *Shrimp and cheese pie*
Broccoli vinaigrette
Butterflake rolls
Lemon sherbet with brownies

SHRIMP AND CHEESE PIE:
Pastry for one-crust 9-inch pie
5 ounces natural Swiss cheese, diced
1 pound shrimp, shelled and deveined
4 eggs
2 cups light cream or half-and-half
Salt, white pepper

Line a 9-inch pie tin with pastry. Bake 5 minutes at 450°. Add shrimp, cheese, and the eggs beaten with cream. Bake 15 minutes. Reduce the temperature to 350° and bake until a knife inserted comes out clean, about 10 minutes more. Serves 4.

SHRIMP AND FISH PIE

A handsome dish for day-in and day-out cooking.

MENU: *Shrimp and fish pie*
Creamed spinach
French fried eggplant sticks
Endive salad
Pears cooked in white wine

SHRIMP AND FISH PIE:
1 9-inch pie shell, baked
1½ pounds codfish steak
½ large onion, sliced thin
6 or 7 cooked shrimp
3 large, fresh mushrooms, sliced thin
4 or 5 slices of lemon
Salt, pepper
1 can frozen cream of shrimp soup

Simmer codfish in a little water with a few pieces of lemon, onion, salt and pepper until fish is opaque (about 5 minutes). The fish should not be overdone. Drain fish, remove any bones, and place in pie shell. Arrange the slices of mushroom wheel-fashion with shrimp in the middle and loops of onion draped around. Dot with butter and pour in shrimp soup. Bake in a medium oven for about 25 minutes. Serves 4.

BUTTERFLY SHRIMP

This, one of the all-time favorite ways of cooking shrimp and eating Chinese, is simple enough to do often.

MENU: *Butterfly shrimp*
Rice
Green beans with chopped black walnuts
Fresh raspberries with sour cream and grated bitter
chocolate

BUTTERFLY SHRIMP:
2 egg whites, slightly beaten
2 tablespoons water
1 teaspoon salt
⅛ teaspoon white pepper
3 tablespoons flour
1½ pounds jumbo shrimp

Mix egg whites, water, salt and pepper together. Add flour
and stir until smooth. Remove shells from shrimp, leaving
tails on. Devein with point of a knife. Slit each shrimp lengthwise almost but not quite through. Spread open and flatten
to make a butterfly shape, dip into the batter and fry until
brown in fat heated to 375°. Drain on paper towels. Serve with
sweet and pungent sauce, or scampi sauce. Serves 4.

SWEET AND PUNGENT SAUCE:
3 tablespoons oil or fat
1 teaspoon salt
Dash of pepper
½ clove garlic, crushed
1 green pepper minced
2 cups bouillon
1 buffet size (8-ounce) can pineapple tidbits
¼ cup sugar
¼ cup vinegar
¼ cup cornstarch
¼ cup water

Heat oil in skillet, add seasoning, garlic and green pepper. Sauté for a couple of minutes, add bouillon, cover tightly and cook a couple of minutes more. Add pineapple, sugar and vinegar and cook 5 minutes longer. Mix cornstarch with water and add to the mixture. Cook 5 minutes or until thickened.

TOMATOES STUFFED WITH CURRIED SHRIMP

This is a light, cool, refreshing dish for a hot day. It may be prepared ahead and chilled in the refrigerator. Serve with spritzers (fill a highball glass with half Rhine wine and half club soda on ice cubes).

MENU: *Tomatoes stuffed with curried shrimp*
Creamed spinach
Noodles amandine
Hot buttermilk biscuits
Black bottom pie

TOMATOES STUFFED WITH CURRIED SHRIMP:
4 medium tomatoes, tops cut off, drained of juice and seeds
1 can (5 ounce) shrimp, crumbled or mashed
⅓ cup mayonnaise
1 tablespoon Madras curry powder
Watercress

Mix shrimp, mayonnaise and curry powder together and spoon into the tomatoes. Chill at least an hour. Serves 4.

SHRIMP REMOULADE

This is one of the classic shrimp dishes found in good restaurants almost everywhere and one that always pleases. It is a specialty of most New Orleans restaurants.

MENU: *Shrimp rémoulade*
Broiled chicken, basted with butter and terragon
vinegar
Noodles amandine
Hot rolls
Lemon curd tarts

SHRIMP RÉMOULADE:
Court bouillon
onions, garlic, sliced lemon, bay leaf, red pepper
and water
1¼ pounds shrimp
2 tablespoons olive oil
2 tablespoons tarragon vinegar
1 teaspoon salt
2 tablespoons mustard
¼ teaspoon paprika
⅓ cup finely chopped celery
1 tablespoon finely chopped parsley
⅓ cup finely chopped onion
1 tablespoon horseradish
2 tablespoons anchovy paste

Make court bouillon by simmering some onion, garlic, lemon, bay leaf, red pepper, and about a quart and a half of water for 10 minutes. Add shrimp and cook until barely pink, not more than 5 minutes. Drain. Make a dressing of oil, vinegar, salt, mustard, paprika, celery, onions, parsley, horseradish, and anchovy paste. Marinate shrimp in this sauce for 12 hours or at least for a long time. Serve on shredded lettuce. Serves 4.

AVOCADO FILLED WITH SHRIMP AND PINEAPPLE

This is a wonderful summer luncheon or supper entrée that is easy to make, cool to serve and quite a spectacular showpiece.

MENU: *Avocado filled with shrimp and pineapple*
Hot biscuits
Angel food cake
Orange and raspberry sherbet

AVOCADO FILLED WITH SHRIMP AND PINEAPPLE:
2 avocados
Lemon juice
2 cups shrimp, cooked, cleaned and deveined
⅔ cup thinly sliced celery
1 can (9 oz.) crushed pineapple, drained
⅔ cup sour cream
1 teaspoon onion salt
⅛ teaspoon salt
¼ cup shredded Swiss cheese

Peel avocados and halve lengthwise. Remove pits. Rub with lemon juice to keep their pretty color. Cut shrimp into ¼-inch pieces. Toss with celery and pineapple. Blend in sour cream, onion salt, salt. Pile salad mixture in avocados and sprinkle each with one tablespoon shredded Swiss cheese. Chill ½ hour before serving. Serves 4.

GRAPEFRUIT AND SHRIMP SALAD

If you want to get back to the simple life after too much heavy food, try this light, sharp and pleasing shrimp salad.

MENU: *Grapefruit and shrimp salad*
French bread
Hot gingerbread with vanilla ice cream

GRAPEFRUIT AND SHRIMP SALAD:
1 cup chilled grapefruit sections, fresh, frozen or canned
2 cans (5 ounce) shrimp, drained, or 1 pound shrimp, cooked, peeled and deveined
⅓ cup diced cucumbers
⅔ cup diced celery
⅓ cup French dressing
Watercress

Toss chilled ingredients together lightly and serve on crisp watercress. Serves 4.

CURRIED SHRIMP SALAD

In my family where strawberry shortcake was taken very, very seriously, the meal preceding it was always light. The biscuits were always large, drop ones about 4-5 inches in diameter and were served hot, spread with butter and filled with crushed and sugared strawberries. More were poured on top with a few whole ones and heavy cream was poured over it. Sometimes it was topped with whipped cream, but not often.

MENU: *Hot mushroom broth*
Curried shrimp salad
Hot poppy seed rolls
Strawberry shortcake

CURRIED SHRIMP SALAD:

1½ pounds shrimp, cooked, peeled and deveined
1 cup white grapes or 1 cup honeydew melon balls
½ cup slivered almonds or chopped walnuts
½ cup mayonnaise or more (enough to blend with the shrimp)
1 to 2 tablespoons Madras or other good curry powder
Watercress
Watermelon pickle

Mix curry powder into mayonnaise and add shrimp and white grapes. Sprinkle nuts on top. Chill well before serving on watercress with watermelon pickle on the side. Serves 4.

SHRIMP AND RAW MUSHROOM SALAD

Raw mushrooms, sliced lengthwise through cap and stems, Japanese fashion, and dressed with olive oil and lemon juice, have a sort of nutty, fresh-picked-from-the-moist-dark-earth-flavor and an intoxicating aroma. The true Italian version of this dish has tiny sea squid called sea strawberries, which are a delight to the unprejudiced palate, included in the ingredients. My countrymen are more squeamish, so scallops are used instead.

MENU: *Cream of tomato soup*
Shrimp and raw mushroom salad
French bread
Key lime pie

SHRIMP AND RAW MUSHROOM SALAD:
  ½ pound raw mushrooms, sliced thin
  Olive oil
  Pepper
  Lemon juice
  (No salt until just before serving.)
  ½ pound cooked shrimp, peeled and deveined
  1 pound bay scallops preferably, or sea scallops cut in
    quarters (Simmer 5 minutes in salted water with
    lemon peel and a slice of onion, drain and cool.)
  1 tablespoon finely chopped parsley
  Watercress

Toss raw mushrooms in olive oil and lemon juice mixture to
which pepper has been added. Then add shrimp, scallops and
parsley. Serve on watercress. Sprinkle with salt just before
serving. Serves 3-4.

SHRIMP AND WILD RICE SALAD

Shrimp are really wonderful. Delicate in themselves and enhanced with delicate seasoning, they are good with lusty flavors
and textures too. Wild rice these days is wildly extravagant.
But a mixture of plain and wild rice on the market is not
prohibitively priced, and some of the flavor and textural con-
trast is present. Aïoli (a sort of garlic mayonnaise) may be
made in seconds in an electric blender.

MENU: *Shrimp and wild rice salad with aïoli*
      Crusty French bread
      Black bottom pie

SHRIMP AND WILD RICE SALAD:

> 1 cup wild rice or 1 cup plain and wild rice mixed
> 1 cup coarsely chopped mushrooms, simmered in
>   butter and cooled
> 2 tablespoons oil
> 2 tablespoons lemon juice
> 2 hard-cooked eggs, yolks sieved and whites coarsely
>   chopped
> 1 green pepper, chopped and seeds removed
> 1 pound peeled, deveined and cooked shrimp
> 1 cup aïoli (p. 174)
> Watercress

Cook wild rice or wild rice mixture in 2 cups water until tender, about 30 minutes. Drain and chill. Dress with the oil and lemon juice. Add shrimp and green peppers and the aïoli. Mix loosely. Sprinkle the top with coarsely chopped egg whites and sieved yolks. Serves 4.

SHRIMP AND TOMATO ASPIC MOLD

On a night when the cook is running behind schedule, and some of the best do, a version of this salad could be concocted with canned tomato aspic, cut in slices and covered with canned shrimp mixed with diced celery and green pepper and tossed with mayonnaise zipped up with a spot of horseradish.

MENU: *Shrimp and aspic mold*
> *Hot biscuits*
> *Ricotta pie with nut crust*
>> (Nut crust filled with ricotta mixed with just enough heavy cream to hold, and citron and shaved chocolate)

SHRIMP AND ASPIC MOLD:
    1 envelope unflavored gelatin
    2 cups tomato juice
    1 chicken bouillon cube
    1 tablespoon lemon juice
    1 package frozen Italian green beans, cooked and
        drained, or 1 avocado, peeled and sliced or
        diced
    1 cup cooked shrimp, canned or frozen

Soften gelatin in tomato juice. Heat with chicken bouillon cube and lemon juice. Chill until the thickness of uncooked egg white. Pour aspic about ½ inch deep in mold to be used. Chill. Arrange the green beans or avocado slices decoratively. Pour another thick layer of aspic and chill. Add the shrimp and the rest of the aspic. (If the aspic thickens before it is all used, heat slightly, chill slightly and use.) Unmold and surround with crisp greens and paper thin slices of lime. This may be molded in one fell swoop but it will not look as if you cared. Serves 4.

AVOCADO RING MOLD WITH SHRIMP

This is a handsome and voluptuous dish, pleasing to the eye as well as the palate. It is tempting and filling on a day when the temperature soars right up into the wild blue yonder.

MENU: *Avocado ring mold with shrimp*
        Hot crescent rolls dipped in melted butter and cracked
            pepper before being heated
        Lemon chiffon pie

AVOCADO RING MOLD:
>   2 envelopes plain gelatin softened in ½ cup cold water
>   1 cup hot water
>   ⅓ cup lemon juice
>   1½ cups grapefruit juice
>   2 teaspoons grated onion
>   2 teaspoons salt
>   3 or 4 drops Tabasco sauce
>   1½ cups puréed or mashed avocado (1 large one)
>   ¼ cup mayonnaise
>   2 cups cooked shrimp, peeled and deveined
>   Watercress
>   1½ cups grapefruit segments

Add softened gelatin to hot water, and stir until dissolved. Add lemon and grapefruit juice, grated onion, salt, Tabasco sauce, puréed avocado and mayonnaise. Pour into 5-cup ring mold and chill until firm. Unmold on a plate and surround with watercress. Fill the center with shrimp and arrange grapefruit segments around the ring on the watercress. No extra dressing is needed. Serves 4 to 6.

COLD SHRIMP MOUSSE WITH WHITE GRAPES AND WATERCRESS

This is a handsome dish for a luncheon or a buffet. It is even pretty enough for a small wedding at home. There is no need for dressing, it's in the mousse.

MENU: *Cold shrimp mousse with white grapes and watercress*
Hot barley and mushroom casserole
Hot rolls
Chocolate éclairs

COLD SHRIMP MOUSSE WITH WHITE GRAPES AND WATERCRESS:
    2 tablespoons gelatin
    ¼ cup dry vermouth
    ½ cup hot orange juice or ½ cup chicken broth
    2 tablespoons lemon juice
    ¼ cup mayonnaise
    1 cup sour cream
    1 tablespoon finely chopped fresh dill or 1 teaspoon
        dill mixture or ½ teaspoon dill seed
    Salt, pepper
    1 pound cooked shrimp, peeled and deveined, or
        2 cans (5 ounce) shrimp, rinsed and drained
    1 cup white grapes
    Watercress

Put the gelatin in the container of an electric blender with vermouth, hot orange juice or hot chicken broth and lemon juice, cover and blend for about ten seconds. Add mayonnaise, sour cream and about half the shrimp. Blend for 1 or 2 minutes, then add the rest of the shrimp and blend until smooth. Remove from blender, stir in white grapes and turn into a 5-cup mold that has been first rinsed in cold water. Chill until firm. Unmold and surround with watercress and whole shrimp, if desired.

It may be made without a blender if shrimp are mashed or put through a food mill or meat grinder using finest blades. Soak gelatin in ¼ cup cold water and then dissolve in vermouth, hot orange juice or chicken broth and lemon juice. Mix with ground shrimp, mayonnaise and sour cream. Stir in the white grapes, turn into a five-cup mold rinsed first with cold water and chill until firm. Unmold on a platter of watercress. Serves 4.

CHARLESTON SHRIMP BREAKFAST

In Charleston, South Carolina, tiny, cold cooked shrimp are served with cold tomatoes and hot hominy and hot biscuits for breakfast. Sometimes shrimp paste is served instead. Shrimp paste is a velvety and voluptuous concoction of ground or mashed shrimp and lots of butter that has chilled long enough for the flavors to have lost their individual identities and become something wondrously new and good. Not only for breakfast, it is good spread on toast and served with cocktails or tea.

MENU: *Cold shrimp or shrimp paste*
Tomatoes peeled and seeded and cut into pieces
Hot hominy
Coffee

SHRIMP PASTE:

1½ pounds shrimp, cooked, peeled and deveined
¼ pound butter
Pinch of mace
½ teaspoon dry mustard
1 teaspoon lemon juice
Salt, pepper
2 tablespoons sherry

Grind the shrimp in a meat grinder, putting it through twice, or put it in an electric blender with the melted butter. If making it in a blender, do half at a time, using half the butter and seasonings, and adding about a cup of shrimp at a time. It is unorthodox to just crumble the shrimp with your fingers, but it is easy and I often do. Whatever method is used, the butter and seasonings are mixed with mashed shrimp and packed in a mold or loaf pan. A regular paté mold is fine, so is a small pottery loaf pan. Chill until needed. This can be frozen if carefully sealed so that other odors do not work their way in. It will keep safely for several months in the freezer, but after about a month or six weeks the flavor seems to deteriorate although the paste is still edible.

POMPANO EN PAPILLOTTE

Pompano is one of America's great seafood contributions to the gastronomy of the world, though mostly people have to come to the United States for it. The delicate filets are best baked in their sauce in parchment or, more conveniently these days, in aluminum foil. Almost any fine sauce tastes well with the delicate flavor of this fish.

MENU: *Pompano en papillotte*
   Tomato soufflé
   Soufflé potatoes (not the same thing at all, but fried potatoes that are hollow like popovers)
   Hearts of artichoke salad
   French bread
   Lemon and angel food dessert

POMPANO EN PAPILLOTTE:
   4 pompano filets
   2 tablespoons chopped green onion
   4 tablespoons butter
   1 can frozen condensed cream of shrimp soup
   1 can (5½-ounce) small shrimp, washed and drained (not obligatory)
   ⅓ cup dry white wine or sherry
   ¼ pound sliced mushrooms

Sauté the onion and filets in the butter until lightly browned on each side. Remove filets from pan. Sauté mushrooms in the rest of the butter until limp. Cut 4 parchment or aluminum hearts about 8 inches long, 12 inches wide, and butter thoroughly. Mix thawed soup and shrimp with cooked onion and wine and put a spoonful in each heart. Lay a filet on top, add more sauce and then some of the mushrooms. Fold half the heart onto the other and crimp the edges in order to seal them. Bake in 450° oven 15 minutes for parchment or 20 minutes for aluminum foil. Serve in the papillotte. Tear open at the table, and let the delicate aroma pour out. Serves 4.

Eight · MIXED SEAFOOD DISHES

BOUILLABAISSE

This dish is fun to shop for and cook and serve, but does sometimes incite some irascible arguments. A. J. Liebling, the writer and food enthusiast, decided once to find out why we couldn't make a bouillabaisse as good as those in Marseille; he found that one of the reasons was we didn't have rascasse. It is a very ugly fish that is tasteless by itself but which acts somewhat as a condimental catalyst. He pursued the subject further than the chefs and the fishermen and went to the ichthyologists who became interested, too. Certainly, we have this fish but we are as a nation squeamish and unadventurous people gastronomically speaking, at least nowadays. Our fishermen shudder when they catch one of these frightful-looking fish and throw it back. "It won't sell, as they say." However, a pleasing mélange of fish and shellfish makes a fine dish.

MENU: *Bouillabaisse*
French bread
Belgian endive
Strawberry cheesecake

168

BOUILLABAISSE:

⅓ cup olive oil
1 clove garlic, minced
1 medium onion, chopped
1 leek, chopped
2 tomatoes, diced, or 1 cup canned tomato pieces
1 cup white wine
1 cup clam juice (bottled)
1 tablespoon chopped fresh fennel, if available, if not,
   1 teaspoon dried
1 bay leaf
½ teaspoon saffron
3 pounds fish, almost any very fresh fish is good, especially red snapper, and, for inlanders, several kinds
   of frozen fillets work well
1 pound uncooked shrimp, peeled and deveined
1 pound scallops
1 small lobster, cut in pieces, or 3 small frozen lobster
   tails, cut in pieces
1 dozen fresh, scrubbed clams in their shells, or 1 can
   clams in their shells in clam juice (the clam juice
   should be strained through cheesecloth)
1 dozen well-scrubbed mussels with beards removed or
   3 fresh blue crabs in their shells or 1 Dungeness
   crab, frozen
2 tablespoons chopped parsley
Salt, pepper

Heat the olive oil in a large deep pot and then add garlic and
onion, leek and tomato. Sauté briefly, then add the wine, clam
juice, fennel, bay leaf and saffron. Simmer for about 15 minutes and add the fish, shellfish and parsley. Cook about 20
minutes longer or until the fish and shellfish are done. Some
fish when fresh should be cooked more briefly than others.

Ask your fishman. For simplicity and ease, serve the fish and shellfish in a tureen or large casserole with the broth. Ladle it over a slice of French bread in each warm soup plate. To be traditional serve the seafood separately on a platter and the broth in a tureen. Serves 6 to 8.

SHRIMP STUFFED WITH SCALLOPS

It may seem a bit silly to stuff shrimp but the combination of flavors and textures does appeal.

MENU: *Shrimp stuffed with scallops*
Baked potatoes
Fresh asparagus with butter
Butterflake rolls
Lemon sherbet with canned orange segments

SHRIMP STUFFED WITH SCALLOPS:
12 cooked jumbo shrimp
3 tablespoons finely chopped bay or sea scallops
⅓ cup Chablis
½ cup cracker meal
1 teaspoon paprika
2 tablespoons crushed potato chips
2 tablespoons freshly grated Parmesan cheese
2 tablespoons melted butter
Watercress
Lemon slices

Peel the shrimp carefully in order to leave as much of the tail as possible. Devein and cut in half, lengthwise, and scoop a little of the shrimp out to make room for the dressing. Mix chopped scallops with Chablis, cracker meal and potato chips. Arrange the stuffing on the slightly hollowed out shrimp.

Sprinkle with grated Parmesan cheese and melted butter and arrange the stuffed shrimp in a shallow baking dish. Bake about 20 minutes. Garnish with watercress and lemon slices. Serves 4.

FRUITS DE MER

At Madame Prunier's in London, there is a wonderful hors d'oeuvre that consists of all the small shellfish except oysters, served on a deep plate of crushed ice. There are tiny shrimp, clams in the shell, steamed mussels, and Dublin Bay prawns. They are served with lemon quarters; very dark pumpernickel and unsalted butter is handed around with them.

MENU: *Fruits de mer*
Veal picatta
Green beans amandine
Tomato aspic with hearts of artichoke
*Ring of sponge cake filled with strawberries and
whipped cream*

CIOPPINO

Cioppino, a glorious mélange of good things from the Western Seas, is claimed as an original dish by the Californians. Without wishing to deny their claim, cioppino does bear a family resemblance to the equally fine Italian Zuppe di Pescia.

MENU: *Cioppino*
Tossed salad
Garlic bread
Mixed cheeses with more French bread

CIOPPINO:

⅓ cup olive oil
1 clove garlic, minced
1 large or 2 small onions, chopped
1 green pepper, chopped
2 tablespoons chopped parsley (preferably Italian
   large-leaf)
1 bay leaf
1 large can (1 pound, 12 ounces) Italian tomatoes
1 pint clam broth
1 dozen clams in their shells, scrubbed
1 pound fish, cut in chunks (bass, croaker or cod)
3 or 4 East Coast blue crabs or 2 West Coast crabs
   or 1 large or 2 small lobsters, cut in pieces (Obviously for the squeamish such as I, these must
   be partially cooked or done by the fishman.)
1 pound shrimp, in their shells
1 teaspoon freshly ground black pepper
½ teaspoon oregano
1½ cups red table wine
   Salt, if necessary; the seafood and clam broth
   have lots.

Sauté garlic, onions, green pepper and parsley in the olive oil
for 3 or 4 minutes or until wilted and partly cooked. Add
Italian tomatoes, bay leaf and clam broth. Bring to a boil,
turn down and simmer for 5 to 10 minutes. Add seafood;
simmer for 10 to 15 minutes more. Add the wine, pepper and
seasonings. Simmer for 3 minutes longer. Pour into a warmed
tureen and serve in large soup bowls with extra plates for the
shells. This serves 8 lusty appetites.

BOURRIDE RAPHAELOISE

It is admittedly sneaky to introduce a bourride, that wonderfully bland, garlicky and creamy fish soup into a book on shellfish. It is not essential that there be shellfish in a bourride, but there can be and it is quite possibly my favorite of all fish soups and perhaps of any kind of soup. In the version called *la veritable bourride Raphaeloise,* the soup is embellished with red eggs from sea urchins or orsini. We have these along our Atlantic Coast in such disparate parts as Maine and Florida, but most natives do not gather or eat them. Sea urchins come into New York at the rate of about 300,000 pounds a year, and may be obtained by ordering a day or so ahead from some fishman. Otherwise use shrimp for garnishing. This soup is unexpectedly filling.

MENU: *Bourride Raphaeloise*
Broiled steak
Cherry tomatoes
Bibb lettuce with French dressing made with lemon juice
Pineapple halves filled with fresh fruits
Chocolate leaves

BOURRIDE RAPHAELOISE:
1 stalk celery, chopped
1 onion, sliced
½ bay leaf
4 or 5 whole peppercorns
Pinch of cayenne pepper
Fish trimmings or 4 cups clam broth
1 pound fish fillets (see next page)
1 cup aïoli
4 slices French bread, toasted
Red eggs of sea urchins or tiny shrimp, cooked and cleaned

Simmer celery, onion, bay leaf, peppercorns and cayenne pepper with fish trimmings in 4 cups water, or clam broth, for 15 minutes. Poach fillets in strained seasoned broth and remove. Stir broth gradually into the aïoli, beating with a whisk or rotary beater until smooth and blended. Pour into warm soup bowls over a slice of toasted French bread. Put a piece of fillet in each bowl and top with red eggs of sea urchins or with tiny cooked shrimp. Serves 4.

AIOLI: (made in a blender)
    2 cloves garlic
    1 egg
    ½ teaspoon dry mustard
    ½ teaspoon salt
    2 tablespoons vinegar
    1 cup salad oil or part olive oil, part salad oil

Put garlic, egg, mustard, salt, vinegar and ¼ of the oil in blender container. Cover and blend at low speed. Remove cover and pour in remaining oil while the motor is going. When oil has all been added, the aïoli is done.

If you have not a blender, add juice from two cloves of garlic, squeezed in a garlic press, to 1¼ cups of commercial mayonnaise and stir well.

ZUPPA DI PESCIA

The Italian version of a bouillabaise.

MENU: *Zuppa di pescia*
    Cooked rice
    Tossed green salad
    Baked apple dumplings

ZUPPA DI PESCIA:

4 tablespoons olive oil
2 cloves garlic
2 pounds fish fillets (flounder, cod or halibut), fresh or
    frozen
1½ dozen littleneck clams (in shells), well-scrubbed
1 dozen mussels (in shells), well-scrubbed
½ pound shrimp, shelled and cleaned
1 can tomato sauce
½ cup chopped parsley
Salt and pepper

Cover bottom of a heavy skillet generously with olive oil. Toss
in 2 cloves garlic cut in half. Add fish, clams, mussels, shrimp,
and tomato sauce. Sprinkle parsley over all and salt and pepper
to taste. Cover tightly, put over medium flame and simmer for
15 minutes. In this time, clams and mussels should open. Simmer for 30 minutes more, basting frequently with juices in the
pan. Cover skillet after each basting. Serve in large deep bowls
over cooked rice. Serves 6-8.

NEW ORLEANS SEAFOOD GUMBO

There are few certainties in life and very few as to the ingredients in a New Orleans gumbo. There must be okra and
gumbo filé (a seasoning made from sassafras and used first by
the Indians). It will be hotly seasoned and always was served
with a separate bowl of flaky rice that was spooned into the
gumbo. Now with the passion for one-dish meals that has
overtaken so many, the rice is cooked right in the stew.

MENU: *New Orleans seafood gumbo*
    French bread
    Pears with chocolate sauce

NEW ORLEANS SEAFOOD GUMBO:

⅓ cup olive oil

4 cloves garlic, minced

1 pound fresh okra

1 green pepper, chopped

1 bunch parsley, chopped

1 heart of celery, tops and bottom, chopped

3 large onions, coarsely chopped

½ pound cooked ham, cubed

1 cup red wine

2 pounds uncooked shrimp, peeled and deveined

1 pound crab meat or 4 hard-shell crabs, steamed, cleaned, the bodies halved and the big claws added

½ cup rice

1 tablespoon Worcestershire sauce

1 teaspoon margarine

1 tablespoon gumbo filé powder

Salt, pepper

Sauté garlic and onion in olive oil. Transfer to a large Dutch oven or enamel pan (2 gallon size). Add all other ingredients, except the seafood and filé. Add 2 cups of water. Simmer about 1 hour. Then add the seafood and cook 30-40 minutes more. This is longer than shrimp or crab need to be cooked, but not too long for them to add their flavor to the dish. Add a cup more water at a time if the mixture starts to boil down. Usually about a quart of water is needed, but it depends on the stove. Just before serving, add the gumbo filé, but do not let it cook. The consistency at the end should be stewlike rather than souplike. Serves 6 to 8. Do not make this dish for a couple of people.

PAELLA

Spanish paella like most other fine regional dishes presumably was based on what was plentiful and available. Even that varied with the seasons and with local conditions. Each cook adapted the dish to suit the likes and dislikes of her family and, of course, the family finances. That is why there is no hard and fast rule for making paella. There should indeed be chicken and sea food cooked in tomato sauce with rice and flavored with the hot Spanish sausage called chorizo, but a chef who cooks for the U.N. uses a sweet sausage. It is also a personal decision about how much clutter you want in the dish. I like to peel the shrimp beforehand, but include the mussels in their shells when I can buy fresh ones because they are so beautiful. It is possible to buy clams in their shells in cans and frozen crab legs for those who live inland but like a dramatic look to the dish. It is difficult for this dish not to look dramatic in whatever large shallow dish you have chosen to serve it in. It may be cooked in one dish and served in another. Paella being such an all-inclusive dish needs little else except perhaps a bland dessert or fresh fruit and coffee.

MENU: *Paella*
French bread, in large amounts
Crème brulée

PAELLA:
3 tablespoons olive oil
1 clove garlic, minced
2 onions, chopped
1 teaspoon oregano
1 2-pound chicken, cut up for frying (no back or wings)
1 large can (1 lb. 12 oz.) tomatoes
Salt
3 tablespoons finely chopped parsley
1 chorizo (hot Spanish sausage), cut in inch pieces
1/5 pound ham, diced

2 packages yellow rice (5 ounces each) or 1½ cup white
rice plus ½ teaspoons saffron
1 cup cooked fresh or frozen green peas
1 can artichoke hearts, drained, or 1 package frozen
artichoke hearts, cooked and drained
1 pound shrimp, peeled and deveined
1 dozen clams in their shells, well scrubbed, or canned
whole ones with or without shells
1 dozen mussels in their shells, well scrubbed and
bearded
1 can pimientos

Sauté garlic and onions in olive oil in a large skillet. Add
oregano and pieces of chicken and brown lightly on all sides.
Transfer chicken, garlic and onion to a large shallow casserole
or paella pan or continue cooking in the skillet. It must be a
large one. A large Dutch oven will do although iron darkens
tomatoes. Add the tomatoes, salt, parsley, chorizo cut in inch
pieces, ham, yellow rice (or plain rice with saffron) and two
cups water. Bring to a boil, then turn heat down very low and
cook for about 20 minutes when the liquid should be absorbed
and the rice tender. Fluff with a fork and cook slightly longer
if necessary. Add shrimp, mussels and clams about 10 minutes
before the rice is done if serving in the pan. If not, cook
shrimp in the sauce and rice, and steam the clams and mussels
separately to use as a garnish. Add more salt and sprinkle the
rice mixture with green peas and arrange shrimp, clams and
mussels artfully. Tuck pieces of pimiento into strategic places
and serve with pride. Serves 6 to 8.

SEAFOOD RABBIT

This may be made with any sort of shellfish, fresh, frozen, or
canned.

MENU: *Seafood rabbit*
Toasted English muffin halves
Orange and grapefruit segments with watercress and French dressing
Angel food cake with sherbet

SEAFOOD RABBIT:

4 tablespoons butter
4 tablespoons flour
1½ cups milk
Salt, pepper
1½ cups grated cheddar cheese
2 cans (5 ounce) shrimp, or crab meat, or lobster, or a mixture of any two

Melt butter and stir in flour. Cook for a minute or two before adding the milk slowly, stirring constantly until smooth and thickened. Add cheese and stir until melted. Stir in seafood and heat. Serve in four individual casseroles, putting under the broiler for a minute or two before serving. Serves 4.

SEAFOOD CREPES

Almost any kinds of shellfish in almost any proportions are delectable when sauced and rolled in thin French pancakes. They are good either as a first course or in larger servings as a main course. The crêpe batter is better when it has stood for two or three hours in the refrigerator before baking and is, of course, made without any sweetening.

MENU: *Seafood crêpes*
Fresh asparagus
Cold braised celery root
French bread
Macaroon soufflé

SEAFOOD CREPES:

2 cups flour
½ teaspoon salt
4 eggs, beaten slightly
1 cup milk
1 cup water
½ cup melted butter
Vegetable oil

Add beaten eggs gradually to sifted flour and salt in a mixing bowl, beating with a wire whisk. Add milk, and water, a little at a time, beating well after each addition. When smooth, add melted butter and stir well. Let stand for two or three hours in the refrigerator. The batter should be about the thickness of thin cream, and just coat a wooden spoon. If it is too thick, add a little water about a tablespoon at a time. (Flours vary according to brand and moisture in the air.) Heat a small skillet or crêpe pan and brush lightly with oil. When the thin film of oil seems to be smoking, pour in three or four table-spoons of batter and tip skillet this way and that so that the batter forms a thin layer. It must be poured and the pan tilted at once or the crêpe gets too thick. Let the crêpe cook about 45 seconds, shaking the pan so that it doesn't stick. When lightly browned, turn over and cook even more briefly on the other side. When finished, slip onto a plate and keep warm while making the rest. They should be about 1/16 of an inch thick. Add more oil and keep on until all are made. Makes 12 to 14 crêpes.

FILLING:

3 tablespoons butter
3 tablespoons flour
1½ cups half-and-half
Salt, pepper

¼ cup sherry
1 tablespoon minced fresh tarragon or 1 teaspoon
   dried tarragon
2 cups mixed cooked shellfish (shrimp, scallops, or
   lobster, any or all)
¼ cup freshly grated Parmesan cheese

Melt butter, blend in flour and cook until almost dried. Add the half-and-half, a little at a time, cooking over low heat and stirring constantly until smooth and thickened. Add the seasonings and sherry. Stir in the seafood; any pleasing combination may be used. Place a tablespoonful on each crêpe and roll. Place side by side in a shallow casserole. Sprinkle with grated Parmesan and heat in a 350° oven until warm and lightly browned. Serves 4 with 3 crêpes per person.

PIERRE'S LOBSTER AND SHRIMP A L'AMERICAINE

Hubert Wrenn, the chef at Pierre's Restaurant, does not use frozen shrimp soup, but thinks it fine for home cooks.

MENU: *Pierre's lobster and shrimp à l'Américaine*
   Wild rice
   Spinach soufflé
   Cherry tomatoes
   French bread
   Chocolate angel pie

PIERRE'S LOBSTER AND SHRIMP A L'AMÉRICAINE:
   ¾ pound cooked lobster, cut in pieces
   ¾ pound shrimp, cooked and peeled
   1 can frozen, condensed cream of shrimp soup
   2 tablespoons Italian tomato paste

½ teaspoon freshly chopped tarragon or ¼ teaspoon
dried tarragon
¼ cup brandy
½ cup sherry

Heat together about 15 minutes over low heat or until just
hot. Do not overcook. Serve on wild rice. Serves 4.

SEAFOOD CASSEROLE

Simple and serenely satisfying.

MENU: *Seafood casserole*
Purée of peas
Hot Parker House rolls
Chocolate roll with whipped cream filling

SEAFOOD CASSEROLE:
½ pound scallops
½ pound fresh mushrooms, sliced
½ pound raw shrimp, peeled and deveined
¼ cup butter
½ cup heavy cream
2 tablespoons sherry or brandy
2 tablespoons finely chopped chives or parsley
Salt, pepper
Bread crumbs

Sauté scallops, shrimp and mushrooms in butter until barely
cooked. Put in a casserole with the juices and butter from the
pan. Add cream, sherry or brandy, chives, salt and pepper.
Sprinkle top with bread crumbs. Dot with more butter and
put in a 350° oven for 20-25 minutes. Serves 4-6.

FILLETS OF SOLE MARGUERY

A streamlined version of this classic dish which does not taste streamlined, or as if the steps that make the dish good were slurred over.

MENU: *Fillets of sole Marguery*
Broiled tomato halves, with butter and chives
Risi pisi
French bread
Tangerine fritters with custard sauce

FILLETS OF SOLE MARGUERY:
4 sole fillets, fresh or frozen
Juice of 1 lemon
1 tablespoon melted butter
1 dozen tiny shrimp, cooked, peeled and deveined
1 dozen oysters, simmered in their own juice until the edges ruffle
1 can frozen condensed cream of shrimp soup
2 tablespoons sherry

Simmer sole fillets in melted butter and lemon juice until the fish is opaque. Arrange in a small, shallow baking dish. Sprinkle shrimp and oysters around and over fillets. Spoon cream of shrimp soup over the dish and sprinkle with sherry. Heat in a 325° oven for about 15 minutes. Serves 4.

SHRIMPS AND SCALLOPS IN CURRIED CREAM

A fine, filling and fattening dish.

MENU: *Shrimps and scallops in curried cream*
Spinach soufflé
Rice pilaff
Hot biscuits
Apricot fritters

SHRIMP AND SCALLOPS IN CURRIED CREAM:
1 pound backfin or lump crab meat
1 pound medium raw shrimp, peeled, deveined and
simmered in butter and white wine 3-5 minutes
1½ cups half cream and half milk
1 teaspoon Madras curry powder
½ teaspoon dill weed
1 jigger of bourbon
⅓ cup white grapes
Salt, pepper

Pick over crab meat and arrange in a shallow buttered casserole with sautéed shrimp. Mix the half-and-half with curry powder, dill weed, whiskey, salt and pepper. Pour this mixture over seafood and sprinkle the top with white grapes. This may be assembled ahead of time and refrigerated. If so, bring to room temperature before baking or allow 10-15 more minutes. Otherwise, bake in a 350° oven 20-25 minutes. Serves 6-8.

BAKED OYSTERS AND SHRIMP AU GRATIN

An elaboration of scalloped oysters.

MENU: *Baked oysters and shrimp au gratin*
Barley casserole
Italian pepper salad (roasted, skinned green peppers
with French dressing)
Hot poppy seed rolls
Pineapple chunks and blueberries with Cointreau

BAKED OYSTERS AU GRATIN:
　　1 quart fresh oysters and juice
　　½ pound small fresh mushroom caps
　　4 tablespoons butter
　　3 tablespoons flour
　　1½ cups half cream, half milk
　　3 tablespoons dry white wine
　　Salt, pepper
　　¼ pound finely slivered natural Swiss cheese
　　½ pound shrimp, cooked, peeled and deveined, or 1
　　　　can (5 ounce), rinsed and drained
Sauté mushrooms briefly in 1 tablespoon butter until partly cooked but not brown. Remove, add the rest of the butter, sprinkle with the flour and stir awhile before adding the half-and-half a little at a time. Stir constantly while adding until the sauce is smooth and thickened. Add white wine and blend. Add seasonings, cheese, oysters, mushrooms and shrimp and bake at 350° 15-20 minutes. Serves 4.

CHESAPEAKE PIE

A deep dish seafood pie traditionally made with seasoned layers of crab meat and oysters, but which tastes equally good with any other combination of shellfish, say, shrimp and clams, mussels and crab meat, appropriately seasoned. The dish this is baked in must be two inches or so deep, and for this purpose a casserole or soufflé dish will do. Traditionally the top crust was decorated with a ring of balls made of chopped oysters, bread crumbs, and mashed hard-boiled egg yolk, seasoned with salt, pepper, mace and nutmeg and fried in butter.

MENU:　*Chesapeake pie*
　　　　Cucumber aspic
　　　　Honeydew melon

CHESAPEAKE PIE:

Pastry, enough for a two-crust 9-inch pie and a single-crust 9-inch pie (There may be a little left over, but one batch is not enough.)
1 pound crab meat, picked over
¼ teaspoon red pepper
1 tablespoon grated lemon peel
3 hard-boiled egg yolks, mashed
1 stick butter
1 pint oysters, drained
Salt, pepper
1 pinch mace
1 pinch nutmeg
½ stick butter
4 tablespoons flour
1 cup oyster liquor
1 cup cream or milk

Line casserole or soufflé dish with pastry. Put half of crab meat in a layer on the bottom. Mix red pepper, lemon peel, egg yolks, and 1 stick of butter. Sprinkle half of mixture on top of the crab meat. Then make a layer of half the oysters. Cream together ½ stick butter, salt, flour, pepper, mace and nutmeg. Crumble half of this over oysters. Put another layer of crab meat and its butter mixture, then add the rest of the oysters and their butter mixture. Mix oyster liquor and cream together and pour over seafood in casserole. Cover with the top crust and put in an oven preheated to 425°. Bake 25 minutes, until crust is well browned. Serves 8.

SEAFOOD QUICHE

Quiches appeal these days to almost everyone, including men who do not otherwise care for smooth and bland dishes.

MENU: *Seafood quiche*
Cucumber and green beans
Melba toast
Fruit compote

SEAFOOD QUICHE:

1 unbaked 9-inch pastry shell
2 cups light cream
4 eggs, beaten
1 tablespoon flour
Pinch cayenne
2 tablespoons cognac
1 teaspoon chopped fresh tarragon
1 tablespoon finely chopped chives
2 cans smoked oysters, drained and chopped
1 cup tiny shrimp, cooked, peeled, and deveined

Beat cream, eggs, flour, salt, cayenne and cognac until well blended. Arrange drained, chopped smoked oysters and shrimp on the pastry shell. Pour cream and egg mixture over it and bake in oven preheated to 375° for about 40 minutes, or until a knife inserted comes out clean. Let stand about 20 minutes before serving. Serves 6.

CHEF'S SALAD OF SEAFOOD

Nino, at the Drake Hotel in New York, serves this salad during Lent and on Fridays. I, who love seafood, serve it whenever the fancy moves me. It is a good warm weather dish, filling but not too fattening. The proportions vary.

MENU: *Chef's salad of seafood*
French bread
Watermelon filled with small fruits

CHEF'S SALAD OF SEAFOOD:
>Romaine, escarole, lettuce, watercress, raw spinach
>Sliced celery
>Crabmeat, flaked and membranes removed
>Shrimp, cooked, peeled, deveined and split butterfly
>   fashion
>Cheddar or imported Swiss cheese, cut julienne
>   fashion
>Olive oil
>Wine vinegar
>3 drops of Maggi seasoning
>Salt, freshly ground black pepper

Toss the greens, celery, crabmeat, shrimp and cheese together lightly. Anoint this with a bland French dressing, 4 parts olive oil to 1 of vinegar, Maggi seasoning, salt and pepper. Serve immediately. Obviously this serves as many as you wish. Allow about a ½ cup seafood and ½ cup torn greens for each serving.

COLD SEAFOOD PLATTER

In these days of plentiful and varied frozen foods there is no reason why any inlander cannot know or have the rich and abundant maritime plenty known as a Cold Seafood Platter. There should be at least three kinds of shellfish and some potato salad served with sliced tomatoes on the largest-sized plate. One of Baltimore's oldest seafood restaurants serves a platter of lobster, lump crab meat and shrimp, but any favorite combination would do. See under the individual shellfish how to boil or broil.

MENU: *Cold Seafood Platter*
          Lobster
          Lump crabmeat
          Shrimp
        Potato salad
        Sliced tomatoes with chopped parsley
        Hot rolls
        Irish coffee

HOT MARINER'S PLATTER

To those who care for seafood, a mariner's platter can be as tempting as a private smörgåsbord and what you put on it in these days of richly varied frozen seafood depends on which ones you like, not on what is available in your coastal regions. Usually, for hot platters, crab cakes, scallops, and so on are deep fried. For individual recipes look under the separate shellfish headings.

MENU: *Hot Mariner's Platter—crab cakes, fried scallops, fried*
          oysters, fried shrimp, fillet of sole
        French fried potatoes
        Cole slaw
        Hot corn muffins
        Honeydew melon

Nine · MISCELLANEOUS SHELLFISH

SNAILS WITH BUTTER

One may start from scratch with live snails, but they have to be purged for several days and there are all sorts of goings-on. Even though snails are the symbol for slowness, they are not sitting still while being purged, but climbing to the top of the lid of the bowl and doing other rather unsettling things. As I have said, I like my food immobile, so I buy snails in cans, with shells packaged on the side. The French even make and export an instant snail mixture, but that seems to be going too far.

MENU: *Snails with butter*
Pork loin stuffed with apricots
Spoonbread
Romaine, tomato, spring onion and cucumber salad
Pears with cheese

SNAILS WITH BUTTER:
2 dozen snails and their shells or little stone pots

SNAIL BUTTER:

6 tablespoons unsalted butter, softened
1 tablespoon minced parsley
1 tablespoon minced chives
2 cloves garlic, finely chopped
1 shallot, finely chopped
1 strip bacon, finely chopped
Lemon juice
Salt, pepper

Mix the butter with herbs, bacon, salt, pepper and lemon juice, blending thoroughly. Put snails in their shells or little stone snail pots and put a little of the butter mixture in each. Place in snail pans or pie tins and heat in the oven at 400° 6-8 minutes or until bubbling hot. Serve immediately. Serves 2-4.

SEA URCHINS

Sea urchins, looking like marine pincushions, may be "hunted" off the Florida East Coast, but they are not commercially fished there. (Not enough demand.) They do come into the New York City markets from Maine, as much as 300,-000 pounds a year and are eagerly bought by the French, Italians, Spanish and the English. They are usually served raw, three or four to a plate, but sometimes they are lightly boiled like an egg. The top is sliced off, the center part removed, and the yellow to pinkish roe that is around the inside of the sea urchin is eaten with a spoon, or it is dipped out and served on small pieces of buttered toast, with dry white wine, to make an unusual first course. They are also made into a purée for filling little puff paste cases or used as filling for an omelet.

MENU: *Sea urchins*
Broiled lamb chops skewered around with kidneys
Barley pilaff
Cold artichokes
Orange Soufflé

PERIWINKLES

These little sea snails are much esteemed abroad and much too little here. In English novels they were boiled in the shell and then picked out with a pin. They are available in large coastal cities like New York and on the Connecticut coast, and those with a foreign background love them. In New York, there are baskets of them outside shops on Mulberry Street. The preparation of periwinkles is very simple. Scrub them and boil for 20 minutes in salted water.

MENU: *Periwinkles*
Spaghetti with meat sauce
Tossed green salad
Italian bread
Spumoni

FLORIDA CONCH CHOWDER

The shell of the conch is one of the most beautiful of all beautiful shells, a spiral one with an iridescent lining that seems mostly pink, the kind that you put to your ear to hear the ocean roar. The conch itself, pronounced "conk" by Floridians and neighboring Bahamians, is not so handsome and is rather tough unless given knowing care. It must be trimmed of its tentacles, and then ground, pounded or pressure cooked. For those with curiosity and the persistence to follow through, it makes a lusty stew, somewhat like a Manhattan clam chowder with a less insistently sea flavor. Italians, who love all kinds of seafood, call this *scungilli*, cook it much the same way but with less liquid and no potatoes. It is then called *scungilli marinara*. It can be bought canned in stores specializing in Italian food. Both Floridians and Italians cut conch in pieces and fry it, serving it with scrambled eggs or as an omelet filling. In Nassau, it is used in salad. In Haiti, the parboiled conch is sometimes cut in pieces and sautéed in butter, lemon juice and garlic.

MENU: *Florida conch chowder*
      Cornbread
      Curly endive with grapefruit segments and French
        dressing
      Chocolate éclairs

FLORIDA CONCH CHOWDER:
    4 conchs, tentacles and black part trimmed off, cut in
      ½ inch pieces
    3 tablespoons olive oil
    1 clove garlic, minced
    1 small onion, chopped
    1 stalk celery, chopped
    ½ large green pepper, chopped
    1 bay leaf
    ½ teaspoon oregano
    ½ teaspoon basil
    2 cups canned tomatoes and their juice
    Extra tomato juice
    2 cups diced, peeled potatoes
    Salt and pepper

Cook the conch under 15 pounds pressure in a pressure pan

for 35 minutes, or boil until tender (it may take all day). Transfer conch and juices to an enamel-lined soup pan. Sauté garlic, onion, celery and green pepper in olive oil until wilted and pale yellow but not browned. Put in the soup pot with the conch, seasonings and tomatoes. Simmer for one hour. Add potatoes and tomato juice as needed. Cook for 20 to 30 minutes or until potatoes are tender. The consistency at the end should be that of a stew rather than of a soup. Serves 4.

COQUINA BROTH

Coquinas, the tiny clams that sparkle with rainbow colors on the beaches in the Gulf of Mexico, make the most delicate clam broth in the world, so I am told. I have seen the shells that open up like tiny butterflies, read of them and the broth, and talked with people who have eaten it. But so far, I have not been lucky enough to have any, not having been in the right places. Coquinas do not travel and are not commercially gathered. One needs a fantastic number of them to make a broth, bucketsful. They are gathered in sieves or colanders and washed in sea water as they are collected. It takes about 6 quarts of coquinas to make a quart of broth. Put thoroughly washed coquinas in a kettle and add cold water, not quite enough to cover. Cover the pan and bring contents slowly to a boil, then turn down to a simmer. The shells will open and the tiny clams and clam juice blend with the water to become a subtle broth. Simmer several minutes, stirring occasionally. Pour through a fine sieve or several layers of cheesecloth, and serve either hot or cold as a fine consommé. Marjorie Kinnan Rawlings suggested in her *Cross Creek Cookery* adding 2 tablespoons of thin cream and a small lump of butter to each serving, but most people prefer clear broth. Also called Donax.

MENU: *Coquina broth*
Watercress and endive salad
Danish red pudding

DIAMONDBACK TERRAPIN

At one time there was a law in Maryland that forbade planters from forcing their slaves to eat terrapin more than two or three times a week. Nowadays, only the rich or reckless or dedicated eat it more than two or three times a year. As with all fine foods, the recipes are just a guide or map to show you the way. Much still depends on the way you follow these directions and on the quality of the ingredients. A terrapin should be not too large or too old, and while much of the meat is edible, only part of it is tender. Terrapin is a tedious and troublesome dish to prepare and, of course, may be bought with the meat already picked out. The recipe from the Maryland Club of Baltimore is generally considered, among those who know, to be the best. This is their version: drop the live terrapin in boiling water for about three minutes. With a towel, rub off skin. Clip off toes. Pull out and skin head. Now boil in another pot until soft to the touch, 45-60 minutes for a six-incher. Break shell apart, break legs and joints. Discard intestines and gall bladder (which looks like a green olive). Slice liver small. Wash eggs and set aside. (The male terrapin is never eaten.) Reduce broth from this pot to a broth which will become, when cold, strong jelly and use enough to cover meat being served. Add ¾ pound of unsalted butter per quart of meat. Flavor with salt, cayenne pepper, sherry. To serve, put meat in saucepan, cook 10 minutes with plenty of butter. Sprinkle the eggs on top just before placing on the table.

MENU: *Diamondback terrapin*
Filet mignon
Maryland beaten biscuits
Baked potato
Bibb lettuce salad
Fresh peaches in champagne

SNAPPER STEW

To most people this recipe will be of academic interest only. A snapper is a kind of turtle and the preparation, long and involved and even slightly horrendous. Luckily, if you are in the snapper region, it is possible to buy the meat already prepared.

MENU: *Snapper stew*
Rib lamb chops
Parsleyed potatoes
Watercress salad with sliced orange and onion
Cherry tarts

SNAPPER STEW:

Snapper is displayed in markets in the cleaned shell, the meat cleaned and ready to cook, except that the white inner tubing and gall sack must be removed. The gall sack is deeply embedded on one side of the liver and one should cut carefully to remove it and any of the liver surrounding it that has been discolored. Put shell and meat in a pot with water enough to not quite cover. Add 2 tablespoons of salt and 2 tablespoons of vinegar. Simmer covered until tender. Do not let the water come to a boil or else the meat will become very tough. The time varies all the way from 45 minutes to several hours and it is difficult to estimate ahead of time because the age of the turtle is unknown and also how strenuous a life he has led. The meat must be fork tender. When almost tender, add liver and the eggs, if you are lucky enough to find them. The cooking time for the eggs is about 20 minutes. The white never becomes thick and opaque like that of a chicken egg. When done, remove from pot and cut meat into serving-sized pieces, being careful to remove every bit of bone. Add diced liver and eggs to the meat and put in a bowl with some of the strained cooking liquid. Add ⅓ cup sherry and chill in the refrigerator. Just before serving, heat the slightly jellied snapper meat in the top of a double boiler and again be very careful not to let it boil. In another pan melt 3 tablespoons butter, add 3 tablespoons flour and stir until almost dry. Add 1½ cups of light cream, a little at a time, stirring constantly until smooth and thickened. Add salt and white pepper. Remove from heat and stir in one beaten egg yolk. Add the hot snapper meat, a pinch of cayenne and serve with toast points.

OYSTER CRABS

There are some who eat these tiny crabs alive and crawling. As their name implies, they are found in raw oysters. But while I like many things rare, I do like my food immobile. Oyster crabs are considered a delicacy and I think they are when cooked. At "21" they are fried and served with whitebait, an equally tiny fish, and are rare and costly and choice. Oyster crabs are a dish enjoyed regionally by many and elsewhere mostly by the very rich. If you have through luck or wealth access to a pound of them, dust them lightly with seasoned flour. Fry a few at a time in deep fat heated to 350°. Fry until golden brown. If too many are cooked at one time, they tend to become a sticky mass. A pound serves 4 or more for a meal, more as an unusual hors d'oeuvre. They are very rich.

At the old Murray Hill Hotel in New York City, alas no longer here, they used to put one little oyster crab and a one-inch square of ham in each bowl of oyster stew, to give a delicate and distinctive flavor.

MENU: *Oyster crabs*
French fried zucchini
Belgian endive leaves, dipped in olive oil
French bread
Wine sherbet

ABALONE

Abalone is found only in California and it is against the law to ship it fresh out of the state. It can be found canned. And evasion of law being what it is, some places freeze and reship from Mexico. This is almost a case of locking the stable after the horse has been stolen. For a long time, Caucasians in California did not eat abalone. The West Coast Chinese did in such large quantities that, with the amount they ate and the amount they dried to ship home, they almost depleted the supply before others started to eat it. Only the large muscle foot is eaten, and unless prepared correctly, it is very tough. Abalone is most often served as a steak. Slice the abalone about one-third of an inch thick and beat a bit with a blunt instrument, a wooden mallet or a bottle. The ones bought already cut are usually already tenderized. Allow one to two slices a serving. Dip slices in an egg beaten with one tablespoon of water, and then in bread crumbs. Sauté in butter not more than 2 minutes on each side. Some say a minute or even less. Abalone should be cooked just long enough to get a light amber color on each side. Remove and serve with quartered lemon.

MENU: *Abalone*
Mushroom pie
Celery Victor
Sourdough bread
Cherry shortcake

Index

Mrs. Reardy's shrimp and artichoke casserole, 147-148

Mushrooms

ham, oysters and, in a chafing dish, 83-84

oysters and, 73

puree, with shrimp in puff shells, 123-124

and shrimp

salad, 159-160

in shells, 146-147

in tomato cream, 130

Mussels

in anchovy sauce, 64-65

barquettes, 61-62

Billi Bi soup, 67

cold, in mustard sauce, 66

fried, with skordalia, 69-71

fruits de mer, 171

à la Marinière, 68

media dolma, 62-63

and rice pilaff, 71-72

smoked pudding, 72

snail butter and, 65

stuffed, 63-64

and baked in the Toulouse manner, 69

Greek fashion, 62-63

Mustard sauce

cold Florida stone crabs with, 34-35

cold mussels in, 66

N

Nasi goreng, 139-140

New England clam chowder, 6-7

New Orleans seafood gumbo, 175-176

Noodles Olympia, 100-101

O

Olympia oysters, see Oysters, Olympia

Onions, oysters and, 93-94

Oyster crabs, 197-198

Oyster (s)

angels on horseback, 74-75

baked

Boston style, 89-90

Golden Door, 77-78

with shrimp, au gratin, 184-185

with wine and walnuts, 78-79

Béchamel with truffles, 88-89

beignets, 104-105

Benedict, 85-86

bisque, 80-81

broiled, 74-75

casino, 92-93

deviled, 76-77

fried, 101-102

parmesan, 102-103

fritters, 105-106

ham, mushrooms and, in a chafing dish, 83-84